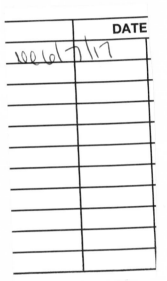
COPY 20

J
BIOG
HAI LE

Negash, Askele.
    Haile Selassie / by Askele Negash. -- New
York : Chelsea House Publishers, c1989.

    111 p. : ill. ; k 7 and up. -- (World
leaders past & present)   93109

    SUMMARY: A biography of the man born Tafari
Makonnen, emperor of Ethiopia during a
forty-four year period, who gave that country
its first written constitution.
    ISBN 1-555-46850-0(lib.bdg.) : $16.95

                                OCT 8 9

    1. Haile Selassie I, Emperor of Ethiopia,
1892-1975.   I. Title.   II. Series.

                                    87-37558 /AC

HAILE SELASSIE

HAILE SELASSIE

Askale Negash

CHELSEA HOUSE PUBLISHERS
NEW YORK
PHILADELPHIA

Chelsea House Publishers
EDITOR-IN-CHIEF: Nancy Toff
EXECUTIVE EDITOR: Remmel T. Nunn
MANAGING EDITOR: Karyn Gullen Browne
COPY CHIEF: Juliann Barbato
PICTURE EDITOR: Adrian G. Allen
ART DIRECTOR: Maria Epes
MANUFACTURING MANAGER: Gerald Levine

World Leaders—Past & Present
SENIOR EDITOR: John W. Selfridge

Staff for HAILE SELASSIE
ASSOCIATE EDITOR: Jeff Klein
COPY EDITOR: Phil Koslow
DEPUTY COPY CHIEF: Ellen Scordato
EDITORIAL ASSISTANT: Heather Lewis
PICTURE RESEARCHER: Kathy Bonomi
ASSISTANT ART DIRECTOR: Loraine Machlin
DESIGNER: David Murray
DESIGN ASSISTANT: James Baker
PRODUCTION COORDINATOR: Joseph Romano
COVER ILLUSTRATION: Alan J. Nahigian

First Printing

1 3 5 7 9 8 6 4 2

Library of Congress Cataloging-in-Publication Data

Negash, Askele.
  Haile Selassie.
  (World leaders past & present)
  Bibliography: p.
  Includes index.
  Summary: A biography of the man born Tafari Makonnen, emperor of
Ethiopia during a 44-year period, who gave that country its first written
constitution.
  1. Haile Selassie I, Emperor of Ethiopia, 1892–1975. 2. Ethiopia—
Kings and rulers—Biography. [1. Haile Selassie I, Emperor of
Ethiopia, 1892–1975. 2. Kings, queens, rulers, etc.] I. Title.
II. Series.
DT387.7.N44 1988   963'.055'0925 [B] [92] 87-37558
ISBN 1-55546-850-0
     0-7910-0685-9 (pbk.)

Contents

John Adams
John Quincy Adams
Konrad Adenauer
Alexander the Great
Salvador Allende
Marc Antony
Corazon Aquino
Yasir Arafat
King Arthur
Hafez al-Assad
Kemal Atatürk
Attila
Clement Attlee
Augustus Caesar
Menachem Begin
David Ben-Gurion
Otto von Bismarck
Léon Blum
Simon Bolívar
Cesare Borgia
Willy Brandt
Leonid Brezhnev
Julius Caesar
John Calvin
Jimmy Carter
Fidel Castro
Catherine the Great
Charlemagne
Chiang Kai-Shek
Winston Churchill
Georges Clemenceau
Cleopatra
Constantine the Great
Hernán Cortés
Oliver Cromwell
Georges-Jacques
    Danton
Jefferson Davis
Moshe Dayan
Charles de Gaulle
Eamon De Valera
Eugene Debs
Deng Xiaoping
Benjamin Disraeli
Alexander Dubček
François & Jean-Claude
    Duvalier
Dwight Eisenhower
Eleanor of Aquitaine
Elizabeth i
Faisal
Ferdinand & Isabella
Francisco Franco
Benjamin Franklin

Frederick the Great
Indira Gandhi
Mohandas Gandhi
Giuseppe Garibaldi
Amin & Bashir Gemayel
Genghis Khan
William Gladstone
Mikhail Gorbachev
Ulysses S. Grant
Ernesto "Che" Guevara
Tenzin Gyatso
Alexander Hamilton
Dag Hammarskjöld
Henry viii
Henry of Navarre
Paul von Hindenburg
Hirohito
Adolf Hitler
Ho Chi Minh
King Hussein
Ivan the Terrible
Andrew Jackson
James i
Wojciech Jaruzelski
Thomas Jefferson
Joan of Arc
Pope John xxiii
Pope John Paul ii
Lyndon Johnson
Benito Juárez
John Kennedy
Robert Kennedy
Jomo Kenyatta
Ayatollah Khomeini
Nikita Khrushchev
Kim Il Sung
Martin Luther King, Jr.
Henry Kissinger
Kublai Khan
Lafayette
Robert E. Lee
Vladimir Lenin
Abraham Lincoln
David Lloyd George
Louis xiv
Martin Luther
Judas Maccabeus
James Madison
Nelson & Winnie
    Mandela
Mao Zedong
Ferdinand Marcos
George Marshall

Mary, Queen of Scots
Tomáš Masaryk
Golda Meir
Klemens von Metternich
James Monroe
Hosni Mubarak
Robert Mugabe
Benito Mussolini
Napoléon Bonaparte
Gamal Abdel Nasser
Jawaharlal Nehru
Nero
Nicholas II
Richard Nixon
Kwame Nkrumah
Daniel Ortega
Mohammed Reza Pahlavi
Thomas Paine
Charles Stewart
    Parnell
Pericles
Juan Perón
Peter the Great
Pol Pot
Muammar el-Qaddafi
Ronald Reagan
Cardinal Richelieu
Maximilien Robespierre
Eleanor Roosevelt
Franklin Roosevelt
Theodore Roosevelt
Anwar Sadat
Haile Selassie
Prince Sihanouk
Jan Smuts
Joseph Stalin
Sukarno
Sun Yat-sen
Tamerlane
Mother Teresa
Margaret Thatcher
Josip Broz Tito
Toussaint L'Ouverture
Leon Trotsky
Pierre Trudeau
Harry Truman
Queen Victoria
Lech Walesa
George Washington
Chaim Weizmann
Woodrow Wilson
Xerxes
Emiliano Zapata
Zhou Enlai

CHELSEA HOUSE PUBLISHERS

ON LEADERSHIP

Arthur M. Schlesinger, jr.

LEADERSHIP, it may be said, is really what makes the world go round. Love no doubt smooths the passage; but love is a private transaction between consenting adults. Leadership is a public transaction with history. The idea of leadership affirms the capacity of individuals to move, inspire, and mobilize masses of people so that they act together in pursuit of an end. Sometimes leadership serves good purposes, sometimes bad; but whether the end is benign or evil, great leaders are those men and women who leave their personal stamp on history.

Now, the very concept of leadership implies the proposition that individuals can make a difference. This proposition has never been universally accepted. From classical times to the present day, eminent thinkers have regarded individuals as no more than the agents and pawns of larger forces, whether the gods and goddesses of the ancient world or, in the modern era, race, class, nation, the dialectic, the will of the people, the spirit of the times, history itself. Against such forces, the individual dwindles into insignificance.

So contends the thesis of historical determinism. Tolstoy's great novel *War and Peace* offers a famous statement of the case. Why, Tolstoy asked, did millions of men in the Napoleonic Wars, denying their human feelings and their common sense, move back and forth across Europe slaughtering their fellows? "The war," Tolstoy answered, "was bound to happen simply because it was bound to happen." All prior history predetermined it. As for leaders, they, Tolstoy said, "are but the labels that serve to give a name to an end and, like labels, they have the least possible connection with the event." The greater the leader, "the more conspicuous the inevitability and the predestination of every act he commits." The leader, said Tolstoy, is "the slave of history."

Determinism takes many forms. Marxism is the determinism of class. Nazism the determinism of race. But the idea of men and women as the slaves of history runs athwart the deepest human instincts. Rigid determinism abolishes the idea of human freedom—

the assumption of free choice that underlies every move we make, every word we speak, every thought we think. It abolishes the idea of human responsibility, since it is manifestly unfair to reward or punish people for actions that are by definition beyond their control. No one can live consistently by any deterministic creed. The Marxist states prove this themselves by their extreme susceptibility to the cult of leadership.

More than that, history refutes the idea that individuals make no difference. In December 1931 a British politician crossing Park Avenue in New York City between 76th and 77th Streets around 10:30 P.M. looked in the wrong direction and was knocked down by an automobile—a moment, he later recalled, of a man aghast, a world aglare: "I do not understand why I was not broken like an eggshell or squashed like a gooseberry." Fourteen months later an American politician, sitting in an open car in Miami, Florida, was fired on by an assassin; the man beside him was hit. Those who believe that individuals make no difference to history might well ponder whether the next two decades would have been the same had Mario Constasino's car killed Winston Churchill in 1931 and Giuseppe Zangara's bullet killed Franklin Roosevelt in 1933. Suppose, in addition, that Adolf Hitler had been killed in the street fighting during the Munich *Putsch* of 1923 and that Lenin had died of typhus during World War I. What would the 20th century be like now?

For better or for worse, individuals do make a difference. "The notion that a people can run itself and its affairs anonymously," wrote the philosopher William James, "is now well known to be the silliest of absurdities. Mankind does nothing save through initiatives on the part of inventors, great or small, and imitation by the rest of us—these are the sole factors in human progress. Individuals of genius show the way, and set the patterns, which common people then adopt and follow."

Leadership, James suggests, means leadership in thought as well as in action. In the long run, leaders in thought may well make the greater difference to the world. But, as Woodrow Wilson once said, "Those only are leaders of men, in the general eye, who lead in action. . . . It is at their hands that new thought gets its translation into the crude language of deeds." Leaders in thought often invent in solitude and obscurity, leaving to later generations the tasks of imitation. Leaders in action—the leaders portrayed in this series—have to be effective in their own time.

And they cannot be effective by themselves. They must act in response to the rhythms of their age. Their genius must be adapted, in a phrase of William James's, "to the receptivities of the moment." Leaders are useless without followers. "There goes the mob," said the French politician hearing a clamor in the streets. "I am their leader. I must follow them." Great leaders turn the inchoate emotions of the mob to purposes of their own. They seize on the opportunities of their time, the hopes, fears, frustrations, crises, potentialities. They succeed when events have prepared the way for them, when the community is awaiting to be aroused, when they can provide the clarifying and organizing ideas. Leadership ignites the circuit between the individual and the mass and thereby alters history.

It may alter history for better or for worse. Leaders have been responsible for the most extravagant follies and most monstrous crimes that have beset suffering humanity. They have also been vital in such gains as humanity has made in individual freedom, religious and racial tolerance, social justice, and respect for human rights.

There is no sure way to tell in advance who is going to lead for good and who for evil. But a glance at the gallery of men and women in *World Leaders—Past and Present* suggests some useful tests.

One test is this: Do leaders lead by force or by persuasion? By command or by consent? Through most of history leadership was exercised by the divine right of authority. The duty of followers was to defer and to obey. "Theirs not to reason why / Theirs but to do and die." On occasion, as with the so-called enlightened despots of the 18th century in Europe, absolutist leadership was animated by humane purposes. More often, absolutism nourished the passion for domination, land, gold, and conquest and resulted in tyranny.

The great revolution of modern times has been the revolution of equality. The idea that all people should be equal in their legal condition has undermined the old structure of authority, hierarchy, and deference. The revolution of equality has had two contrary effects on the nature of leadership. For equality, as Alexis de Tocqueville pointed out in his great study *Democracy in America*, might mean equality in servitude as well as equality in freedom.

"I know of only two methods of establishing equality in the political world," Tocqueville wrote. "Rights must be given to every citizen, or none at all to anyone . . . save one, who is the master of all." There was no middle ground "between the sovereignty of all and the absolute power of one man." In his astonishing prediction of 20th-century totalitarian dictatorship, Tocqueville explained how the revolution of equality could lead to the *"Führerprinzip"* and more terrible absolutism than the world had ever known.

But when rights are given to every citizen and the sovereignty of all is established, the problem of leadership takes a new form, becomes more exacting than ever before. It is easy to issue commands and enforce them by the rope and the stake, the concentration camp and the *gulag*. It is much harder to use argument and achievement to overcome opposition and win consent. The Founding Fathers of the United States understood the difficulty. They believed that history had given them the opportunity to decide, as Alexander Hamilton wrote in the first Federalist Paper, whether men are indeed capable of basing government on "reflection and choice, or whether they are forever destined to depend . . . on accident and force."

Government by reflection and choice called for a new style of leadership and a new quality of followership. It required leaders to be responsive to popular concerns, and it required followers to be active and informed participants in the process. Democracy does not eliminate emotion from politics; sometimes it fosters demagoguery; but it is confident that, as the greatest of democratic leaders put it, you cannot fool all of the people all of the time. It measures leadership by results and retires those who overreach or falter or fail.

It is true that in the long run despots are measured by results too. But they can postpone the day of judgment, sometimes indefinitely, and in the meantime they can do infinite harm. It is also true that democracy is no guarantee of virtue and intelligence in government, for the voice of the people is not necessarily the voice of God. But democracy, by assuring the right of opposition, offers built-in resistance to the evils inherent in absolutism. As the theologian Reinhold Niebuhr summed it up, "Man's capacity for justice makes democracy possible, but man's inclination to injustice makes democracy necessary."

A second test for leadership is the end for which power is sought. When leaders have as their goal the supremacy of a master race or the promotion of totalitarian revolution or the acquisition and exploitation of colonies or the protection of greed and privilege or the preservation of personal power, it is likely that their leadership will do little to advance the cause of humanity. When their goal is the abolition of slavery, the liberation of women, the enlargement of opportunity for the poor and powerless, the extension of equal rights to racial minorities, the defense of the freedoms of expression and opposition, it is likely that their leadership will increase the sum of human liberty and welfare.

Leaders have done great harm to the world. They have also conferred great benefits. You will find both sorts in this series. Even "good" leaders must be regarded with a certain wariness. Leaders are not demigods; they put on their trousers one leg after another just like ordinary mortals. No leader is infallible, and every leader needs to be reminded of this at regular intervals. Irreverence irritates leaders but is their salvation. Unquestioning submission corrupts leaders and demeans followers. Making a cult of a leader is always a mistake. Fortunately hero worship generates its own antidote. "Every hero," said Emerson, "becomes a bore at last."

The signal benefit the great leaders confer is to embolden the rest of us to live according to our own best selves, to be active, insistent, and resolute in affirming our own sense of things. For great leaders attest to the reality of human freedom against the supposed inevitabilities of history. And they attest to the wisdom and power that may lie within the most unlikely of us, which is why Abraham Lincoln remains the supreme example of great leadership. A great leader, said Emerson, exhibits new possibilities to all humanity. "We feed on genius. . . . Great men exist that there may be greater men."

Great leaders, in short, justify themselves by emancipating and empowering their followers. So humanity struggles to master its destiny, remembering with Alexis de Tocqueville: "It is true that around every man a fatal circle is traced beyond which he cannot pass; but within the wide verge of that circle he is powerful and free; as it is with man, so with communities."

1

At the League of Nations

It was the morning of June 30, 1936, in Geneva, Switzerland, headquarters of the League of Nations. The usual collection of diplomats, delegates, and government representatives took their seats in the world body's main hall as the assembly was called to order. A special session had been convened to discuss a problem of the utmost importance.

Suddenly, the attention of the delegates turned to a figure entering through the doors at the back of the hall. Walking slowly and deliberately into the assembly hall was a short, frail man wrapped in a long black cloak, a man with the rigid bearing and dignity of a king. He was gravely handsome, with high cheekbones and chiseled features, a long, delicately aquiline nose, light brown skin, and a curly black beard framing his jaw and mouth. But what fixed the delegates' attention was his eyes — dark and deep set, with a penetrating gaze that seemed to look beyond what was in front of him. The delegates knew who he was: Emperor Haile Selassie of Ethiopia.

It is a choice between the principle of the equality of states and the imposition upon small Powers of the bonds of vassalge.
—HAILE SELASSIE
in his address to the
League of Nations

Emperor Haile Selassie I of Ethiopia stands at the microphone at League of Nations headquarters in Geneva, Switzerland, on June 30, 1936. His speech, in which he appealed to the League to stop Italy's invasion of his country, is today considered one of the most inspired speeches of the 20th century.

Haile Selassie and the Ethiopian delegation at the League's assembly chamber on June 30. The emperor had fled his country when Italian forces overran it two months before. Despite his speech, the League refused to help Ethiopia and recognized the Italian conquest.

As the emperor and his small party of aides, who followed him at a close but respectful distance, took their seats in the fifth row, the session began in an atmosphere of tension. The League was set to debate the imposition of further economic sanctions against Italy for its October 1935 invasion of Ethiopia. The assembly had already imposed some sanctions and condemned the massive Italian invasion and occupation of the East African nation. But it was becoming increasingly clear that France and England were going to push for the repeal of that condemnation in an attempt to keep Italy's Fascist dictator, Benito Mussolini, from allying with Germany's Nazi dictator, Adolf Hitler.

On this crucial day, Haile Selassie was scheduled to address the international body, the first head of state ever to do so. The emperor, accompanied by a few Ethiopian dignitaries and an American adviser, sat quietly in the fifth row awaiting his call to speak.

When the appointed time came, Haile Selassie arose and approached the rostrum. As he took his place in front of the microphone and prepared to speak, a group of Italian newspapermen started screaming obscenities, shocking the assembly. The emperor stood, calmly gazing at the shrieking journalists as though nothing concerning him was going on. Finally, after the Rumanian delegate protested against the Italian journalists' behavior, the president of the assembly ordered the guards to remove them from the hall. Once this was done, quiet was restored.

Haile Selassie then glanced down at his written text and began his address, speaking in Amharic, his native language. To the predominantly European and Latin American delegates it sounded a bit like Arabic, but none of them could understand it. They listened respectfully, but because there was no simultaneous translation they had to wait until half an hour after the completion of the speech before they knew what the emperor had said.

When the translation, into French, was read, the delegates were stung by the emperor's bitter disappointment in them and struck by the dignity with which he expressed it. "I, Haile Selassie the First, Emperor of Ethiopia," he had said, "am here today to claim the justice that is due to my people and the assistance promised to it eight months ago by 52 nations, who asserted that an act of aggression had been committed in violation of international treaties."

The translation continued with the emperor's review of the history of the invasion and of Ethiopia's repeated attempts to resolve the crisis through negotiations and continuous appeals to the League of Nations. He discussed the sorry state of his forces inside Ethiopia, due mainly to the lack of financial aid and to a deliberate arms blockade led by some of the League's member nations. He pointed out that France, which owned the only railroad in the region, was allowing the Italians to use it to transport weapons to the battlefront. He passionately recounted the atrocities committed by Italian forces over the previous eight months, including the massacre of thousands of Ethiopian civilians by poison gas.

> The Ethiopian Government never expected other Governments to shed their soldiers' blood to defend the Covenant. . . . Ethiopian warriors asked only for the means to defend themselves.
> —HAILE SELASSIE to the League

Ethiopian soldiers marching to the front to repel the Italian invasion in March 1936. Ethiopia's forces, led by local and regional noblemen, were poorly equipped, usually with little more than 40-year-old rifles.

The delegates listened closely to the translation of Haile Selassie's indictment of their actions: "I assert that the issue before the assembly today is not merely a question of the settlement in the matter of Italian aggression. It is a question of collective security; of the very existence of the League; of the trust placed by states in international treaties; of the value of promises made to small states that their integrity and independence shall be respected and assured. . . . In a word, it is international morality that is at stake."

A sense of shame became almost palpable among the delegates as they heard what the emperor had said at the conclusion of his speech:

Outside the Kingdom of God, there is not on this earth any nation that is higher than any other. If a strong government finds that it can, with impunity, destroy a weak people, then the hour has struck for that weak people to appeal to the League of Nations to give its judgment in all freedom. God and history will remember your judgment.

Placed by the aggressor face to face with the accomplished fact, are states going to set up the terrible precedent of bowing before force?

I ask the great powers, who have promised the guarantee of collective security to small states, those small states over whom hangs the threat that they may one day suffer the fate of Ethiopia: What measures do they intend to take? Representatives of the world, I have come to Geneva to discharge in your midst the most painful of the duties of the head of state. What answer am I to take back to my people?

The League now knew what Haile Selassie had said when he had stood before the microphone. They were not told that as he had stepped down from the podium he had muttered in Amharic, "It is us today. It will be you tomorrow."

Italian soldiers parade in Rome before Italy's dictator, Benito Mussolini, and king, Victor Emmanuel III, in June 1935, during the buildup that preceded the invasion of Ethiopia. Italy used tanks, airplanes, and poison gas against soldiers and civilians to defeat the Ethiopians, who had no modern weapons.

Italian dictator Benito Mussolini (right) stands next to his German counterpart, Adolf Hitler, in Munich in 1938. The League had failed to act against Mussolini's invasion of Ethiopia in an effort to win his support against Hitler. But he sided with the Nazi dictator nevertheless, an alliance that sparked World War II.

All who were present for Haile Selassie's speech would later agree that it was one of the most moving and effective speeches they had ever heard, and 50 years later it would be widely regarded as one of the great speeches of the 20th century. Yet despite the power and integrity of the emperor's words, the League rejected his appeal. Two weeks after Haile Selassie's speech to the assembly, the League voted to lift its sanctions against Italy. Shortly thereafter, governments around the world, willing to sacrifice an African nation to placate Mussolini, began to extend recognition to the Italian regime in Ethiopia.

The decision to abandon Ethiopia implied that no small nation could expect to be supported and defended by the League of Nations in the event of aggression by a stronger power. The green light was on for Mussolini and Hitler, who reacted to the League decision by proceeding at full speed with their military buildups and their plans to invade neighboring European countries — events that led to the outbreak of World War II. Today most historians believe that the League's decision not to oppose Italy's invasion and occupation of Ethiopia was, in effect, the beginning of the war.

In spite of Haile Selassie's failure to convince the assembly to support his country's cause, the speech at the League of Nations marked a turning point in his life. Haile Selassie was no longer merely the emperor of a poor and isolated African country. He was now a recognized world leader who had dared to speak against fascism. For millions of people around the world, Haile Selassie became a symbol of resistance to the brute force of fascism. He was welcomed by admiring crowds wherever he traveled, and for the next four decades he would be hailed in Europe, Asia, North and South America, and Africa as a visionary leader committed to the cause of justice, progress, and black nationalism. In some places he was even revered as a divine messenger of God.

Five years after the speech in Geneva the Italians would be ousted from Ethiopia, and the victorious emperor would return to his throne. For the next 30 years he would reign with the absolute power of

A government minister bows to Haile Selassie as an attendant looks on in the early 1970s. Haile Selassie ruled Ethiopia as regent from 1916 to 1930 and as emperor from 1930 to 1936. He resumed his reign in 1941 and continued his autocratic rule until 1974, when he was finally overthrown.

a medieval king, holding court and dispensing gifts from a golden cashbox, throwing coins to peasants on trips through his realm, strolling through his menagerie of peacocks and caged lions. His subjects would hurl themselves to the ground whenever he passed, never daring to look him in the eye. Scores of minor officials were employed at his palace, each of them assigned a single, simple function. One of them told a Polish journalist of the emperor's favorite dog:

> It was a small dog, a Japanese breed. . . . During various ceremonies, he would run away from the Emperor's lap and pee on dignitaries' shoes. The august gentlemen were not allowed to flinch or make the slightest gesture when they felt their feet getting wet. I had to walk among the dignitaries and wipe the urine from their shoes with a satin cloth. This was my job for ten years.

In 1974, after ruling Ethiopia for more than 50 years, Haile Selassie was overthrown by the Ethiopian military. Soldiers took him from his palace and drove him through the streets of the capital on the way to confinement in a nearby military barracks. The citizens of the capital, who just a few months earlier had prostrated themselves before him in awe-filled reverence, saw him in the back of the car and shouted, "Thief! Thief!"

In some parts of the world that day, Haile Selassie was still thought to be divine.

2
The Glory of the Kings

Tafari Makonnen — the infant who would grow up to be Haile Selassie I, Emperor of Ethiopia — was born in a round mud-and-wood hut on July 23, 1892, in Ejarsagoro, a small village in Harer province. Tafari's father, a *ras*, or duke, was the governor of Harer, which five years earlier had become the newest province in Ethiopia's expanding empire.

As the infant was born, priests stood in attendance chanting prayers while physicians and servants attended to the mother and child. The servants took the tiny baby, washed him, and gently rubbed his body with oils and butter. The word was passed through the door of the hut that the baby was a boy—and healthy.

Outside, the newborn's father, Ras Makonnen, greeted the news with austere joy. Behind him stood a retinue of soldiers, while farther back a crowd of peasants knelt on the ground, deep in prayer for the health of their duke's heir. Makonnen turned to his men, his sword, pistol, and cartridge belt glinting in the sun, and gave the word; they raised their rifles and fired into the air. As the sound of the shots echoed over the valleys, they were answered by other gunshots far away. Soon, shots were being fired everywhere in the province, celebrating the birth of Tafari Makonnen.

As I grew up the spiritual desire was guiding me to emulate him and so to conduct myself that his example should dwell within me.
—HAILE SELASSIE
on his father

The eight-year-old future emperor of Ethiopia and his father, *Ras* (Duke) Makonnen. Haile Selassie was born Tafari Makonnen in 1892; his father was the powerful governor of Harer province, conquered by the expanding Ethiopian empire in 1887.

A richly adorned mule was led to Ras Makonnen to carry him the few steps from where he was standing to the door of the hut. He dismounted, entered the hut, and saw his son for the first time. Tafari was the tenth child born to Makonnen and his wife, Yishimabet. He would be the only one to survive to adulthood.

The Ethiopia of 1892 was little different from the Ethiopia of centuries before: a poor but fiercely proud nation bound by extraordinarily rigid traditions and ruled by a constantly warring network of kings, princes, dukes, and lords. Perhaps 20 million people — thousands of them slaves — lived within its borders, from the headwaters of the Blue Nile in the north to the deserts and grasslands of the south. Isolated from the rest of the world both by choice and by its rugged geography, the Ethiopian nation was made up of scores of different peoples, some Christian, some Muslim, some Jewish, some holding animist beliefs similar to those found elsewhere in Africa, but all deeply religious. Tafari Makonnen was born a Christian and an Amhara, the dominant ruling ethnic group in Ethiopia.

A typical Harer village, featuring the round, hutlike houses called *tukals* like the one in which Tafari was born in the village of Ejarsagoro on July 23, 1892. The only one of Ras Makonnen and Yishimabet Ali's 11 children to survive to adulthood, Tafari Makonnen's education was entrusted to French missionaries.

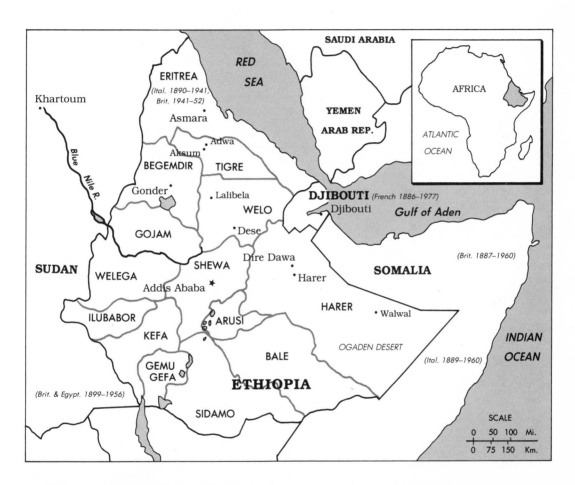

The estimated population of Ethiopia, which has never had a census, was 20 million in 1900 and 46 million in 1988. The mountainous north was long the home of the Amhara kingdoms, but with the conquest of the south in the 1880s and the addition of Eritrea in 1962, Ethiopia is now the size of Spain, France, and Great Britain combined.

A 16th-century Ethiopian painting depicting the crucifixion. Ethiopia, which adopted Christianity around the year 325, had been an independent kingdom since long before the birth of Christ. The only Christian nation in Africa, it was made up of several ethnic groups, the Amhara being the dominant one.

The ancestors of the Amhara came to Africa from the Arabian peninsula sometime around 1000 B.C. They settled in the highlands of what became the northern Ethiopian provinces of Shewa and Tigre. In Tigre, in the 1st century A.D., they founded the kingdom of Aksum by conquering their darker-skinned neighbors. The Amhara were known to the classical Greeks and later to the Roman Empire, which employed the Axumite kingdom as an ally during its wars for control of the Red Sea.

Around 325 the Amhara adopted Christianity, which at that time was rapidly becoming the dominant religion of Europe and the Middle East. The particular form of the religion the Amhara adopted came to be known as Coptic Christianity, which held that Jesus Christ's nature was solely divine. It was a belief that was denounced as heresy 100 years later by most of the rest of the Christian world, but the Amhara and the Coptic Christians of Egypt never abandoned their faith.

The realm of the Axumite kingdom reached from what is today northern Ethiopia across the Red Sea and into southern Arabia, but sometime around 650 the kingdom fell. Shortly thereafter the followers of the new religion of Islam, founded in Arabia, swept through the Middle East and North Africa, thus cutting off the small Amhara kingdoms that remained from the rest of the Christian world. For the next 700 years they lived in relative isolation, their kings engaging in constant warfare among themselves and against their Muslim neighbors.

In 1490 a representative of the king of Portugal, intrigued by stories of a Christian monarch ruling somewhere in Africa, found the Amhara kingdom sheltered in the steep mountains and deep ravines of northern Ethiopia. He returned to Portugal with the Amhara's request for help in combating the Muslims to the north and east; the request was granted, and on various occasions over the next 60 years Portuguese and Ethiopian soldiers fought side by side against Muslim armies. Although they were successful in repulsing the Islamic forces, they could not prevent many Muslim tribes from settling in Amhara territory and maintaining independent dukedoms. In 1633 the Amhara expelled the Portuguese after Portuguese Jesuit missionaries tried to convert the Ethiopian Coptic Christians to Roman Catholicism.

The Ethiopian state began to take on its modern form in the first half of the 1800s, with the reign of Sahle Selassie, *negus*, or king, of the Amhara province of Shewa. Sahle Selassie — the great-great-grandfather of Tafari Makonnen — conquered the surrounding Christian Amhara kingdoms and the nearby dukedoms of the Muslim Oromo peoples. He signed treaties with the British and French, who were occupying nearby lands in preparation for establishing colonies in East Africa.

The death of Sahle Selassie was followed by years of bloody warfare between the armies of various nobles seeking ultimate power — for centuries, this had been the usual procedure in Ethiopia after a king died. Finally, a new negus climbed to the throne: Tewodros II, who crowned himself *negusa negast*, king of kings, or emperor, of Ethiopia, and extended the nation's dominions. In 1868 he refused to release a British ambassador he had taken hostage,

Priests in the ancient city of Aksum, center of the Ethiopian Orthodox Church. The Aksumite kingdom was an ally of the Roman Empire and later controlled parts of Arabia, but it disintegrated with the rise of Islam in the 7th century. The small Amhara kingdoms that survived remained isolated from the rest of the world for 700 years.

prompting Britain to send a military expedition to oppose Tewodros's army. Faced with certain defeat, the Ethiopian emperor committed suicide. The next emperor, Yohannes IV of Tigre, fought other Tigrean and Amhara kings and Egyptian, Italian, and Muslim armies continuously for more than 20 years.

Yohannes was killed in battle in 1889 and was succeeded by Ras Makonnen's friend and cousin, Menilek II, who quickly subdued his rivals for the throne and established firm control over the empire. Menilek conquered Harer in the southeast, and he rewarded Ras Makonnen, a leading general in the conquest of the province, by naming him its governor. In 1890 he sent Makonnen to Rome to negotiate a treaty with Italy, which controlled Eritrea and Italian Somaliland, two territories adjacent to Ethiopia along the Red Sea. Makonnen's mission succeeded and he returned to Ethiopia with thousands of Italian rifles and cannon. But hidden in the Italian text of the treaty was a clause under which Ethiopia handed over to Italy its right to negotiate with foreign governments. Menilek, fearing that such a provision would lead to an Italian takeover of Ethiopia, quietly and successfully sought arms and financial assistance from France, Germany, and Russia, and rejected the treaty with Italy in 1893—just a few months after Tafari was born.

An Ethiopian painting depicting the Queen of Sheba's trip to Jerusalem to meet King Solomon. According to Ethiopian legend, the Queen of Sheba came from the northern province of Tigre; the child she bore after her union with Solomon became Menilek I, the first emperor of Ethiopia.

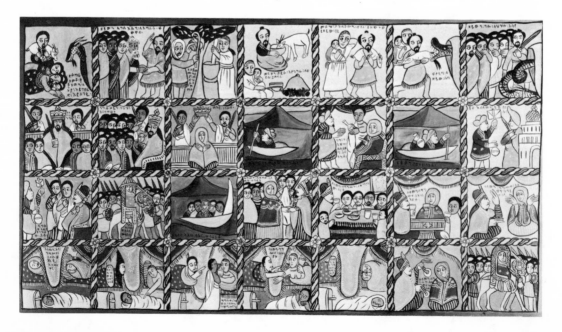

Italy built up its forces in Eritrea and in 1895 invaded Ethiopia. But the 14,000-man army — 9,000 of whom were Italians, with the remainder Eritreans and Somalis — suffered defeats in a series of small battles and was forced to retreat. Italy's prime minister felt that this was a humiliation and ordered the army to renew the invasion. In early 1896 the Italian forces reentered Ethiopia and on March 1 near the town of Adwa encountered Menilek's army: 80,000 Ethiopians, armed with modern rifles and cannon. The ensuing battle was one of the worst defeats ever inflicted by Africans upon a European army, with the Italians losing nearly 10,000 men killed, wounded, or taken prisoner. Soon thereafter, Italy agreed to Menilek's demand that the treaty be annulled and Italian forces be confined to Eritrea.

A 12th-century church in the holy town of Lalibela in Welo province. This and 10 other 700-year-old churches in Lalibela were hewn out of solid rock; this church reached 5 stories into the ground. There are more than 10,000 churches and monasteries in Ethiopia, where approximately 50 percent of the population is Christian.

A recent photo of Ethiopian Jews, who call themselves *Bet Israel* (House of Israel) but who are derogatorily called *Falasha* (Strangers) by Ethiopian Christians. Numbering about 30,000, they are believed to have adopted Judaism before the 6th century and were unknown to the rest of the world until 1900.

The victory at Adwa insured that Ethiopia would remain one of only two African nations never to be conquered by Europeans. The other, Liberia in West Africa, had actually been created by the United States as a haven for freed slaves. Its history as a nation began in 1823; Ethiopia's stretched back to the beginnings of recorded history.

The victorious Menilek was now free to expand his empire to the south. He conquered the arid Ogaden region in 1899 and consolidated the empire's hold on the southwest and west by subjugating the remaining semi-independent Oromos. He also founded Ethiopia's first permanent capital, Addis Ababa (Amharic for "the New Flower"), on a high plateau among the mountains of Shewa, practically in the geographical center of the empire.

Menilek's style of ruling was very much in keeping with the royal traditions of Ethiopia. He handed out money, titles, manors, dukedoms, and provinces to the most faithful and trustworthy of the nobles. Those receiving grants of land were free to run their holdings as their own private fiefdoms as long as they did nothing to undermine the absolute authority of the emperor. The nobles not only owned their lands and a large share of all the crops, domestic animals, and wildlife contained thereon — they were entitled to as much as one-third of the labor of all the people who lived on the land as well.

The Ethiopian nobility had control over the peasantry in much the same way that the lords of medieval Europe or 19th-century Russia had control over their serfs.

Ras Makonnen, perhaps the most loyal and trusted member of Menilek's court, was one of the most powerful men in Ethiopia. The province he governed, Harer, was of great strategic importance to the empire. With Italy in control of Eritrea, leaving Ethiopia totally landlocked, the only available route for the nation's foreign trade was the French-owned railroad that ran through Harer to the French colony of Djibouti on the Red Sea.

Aside from its strategic location, the province was important because it was the first stop for all foreigners headed to Menilek's court to conduct diplomatic or commercial business, as well as for the European adventurers who had come to see the "exotic" Christian empire in the heart of East Africa. The heavy traffic of foreigners almost always stopped at Ras Makonnen's court before proceeding to Addis Ababa, exposing young Tafari to outsiders — an experience shared by only a handful of other Ethiopian nobles.

Very little is known about Tafari's mother, *Woizero*, or Lady, Yishimabet Ali. The beautiful daughter of a minor nobleman from the north, Yishimabet was Makonnen's second wife; they were married in 1876. Tafari was taken from her soon after his birth — perhaps because the death of her previous children left Makonnen nervous about leaving him in her care — and entrusted to the custody of Makonnen's loyal general, Haile Sellassie Abayneh. Yishimabet was never again allowed to see Tafari. There is nothing to suggest that she made any mark on the future emperor's life; years later, he would barely mention her in his autobiography. She died on March 14, 1894, when Tafari was about 18 months old, from complications following the delivery of her eleventh child.

Tafari was raised by General Abayneh and years later remembered him affectionately. The general's son, Imru, was the same age as Tafari and his second cousin as well, and they developed a close bond

A 19th-century lithograph of Emperor Menilek II and his wife, Empress Taitu. Menilek ascended the throne in 1889, stopped the constant warfare between rival nobles, and continued the conquests begun by his predecessor, Yohannes IV, who was killed in battle. Menilek is considered the founder of modern Ethiopia.

An Ethiopian depiction of the March 1896 Battle of Adwa, in which 80,000 Ethiopians destroyed an invading Italian army of 14,000. The victory kept Ethiopia the only major African nation never to have suffered European conquest. Menilek is enthroned at the top left, and St. George, Ethiopia's patron saint, is at top center.

that would last the rest of their. The warmth with which he later described his relationship with General Abeyneh and Imru contrasted with what he felt toward his father: love, but love very much tempered by respect and deference.

The distance between father and son was largely the result of Ras Makonnen's busy schedule, which required him to travel constantly for military campaigns inside the country and as Menilek's unofficial foreign minister. The latter capacity gave him the unique opportunity to travel to foreign countries such as England, which he visited in 1892 to represent Ethiopia for the coronation of King Edward VII. Makonnen's constant travel, especially to Europe, was a mixed blessing for Tafari: Although he could not spend as much time as he would have liked with his only surviving parent, it did lead him to accept the importance of European education.

While Ras Makonnen recognized the importance of contact with European culture for his son, he also knew that Tafari would have to be well-versed in the treacherous life of the *ghibbi*, or palace. Tafari, as a descendant of the Shewan dynasty and the son of Menilek's most trusted lieutenant, had a remote but legitimate claim to the throne. In the ghibbi, Tafari's fortunes — and possibly his life — would depend on his mastery of traditional warfare, his knowledge of the teachings of the Ethiopian Orthodox Church and a good rapport with its bishops, and his absolute loyalty and obedience to the emperor. Most of all Tafari would have to develop the ability to understand court intrigues, quickly and ably, in order to determine which side would win and therefore which side to ally himself with.

Tafari was only four when the Italo-Ethiopian war of 1895–96 broke out. Ras Makonnen left Harer to join the emperor, leaving his delicate son to the care of French missionaries working in the ancient walled city of Harer, the capital of the province. Among Tafari's teachers was a French Roman Catholic missionary priest, Father André Jarosseau, who treated him like a son. Jarosseau taught Tafari in the European manner, including the French language, and would prove to be a close and valuable adviser to the young nobleman for many years to follow.

A 1900 photo of Addis Ababa, the empire's first permanent capital, founded by Menilek early in his reign. Situated 8,000 feet high in the mountains of Shewa province and enjoying an average year-round temperature of 70 degrees, the establishment of Addis Ababa (Amharic for "New Flower") marked the end of the system of moving the capital from place to place with the emperor's travels.

Tafari's formal, Ethiopian education began when he was five years old. He was assigned an Ethiopian teacher who educated him in the traditional manner, which consisted of learning to read and write Amharic. In addition, he learned Ge'ez, the language from which Amharic was derived; the Bible and other sacred books of the Ethiopian Orthodox Church were written in Ge'ez, and it was the language in which church services were still conducted. Such schooling was reserved for the sons of the nobility and the upper classes. The vast majority of Ethiopians never received any organized education of any sort and, as a result, virtually all of them were illiterate.

Although Tafari's first Ethiopian teacher left little impression, his second teacher, Gebre Selassie, did influence the boy's character to a great extent. Gebre Selassie was a monk from the northern province of Gojam, known as the center of learning for the Ethiopian Orthodox Church. He was deeply committed to teaching his student not only the basic traditional subjects, but also the moral values associated with Coptic Christianity and the Amhara aristocracy: respect for elders, skill at oratory, absolute obedience to superiors within the rigid structure of the traditional hierarchy, and all the other virtues expected from a good Christian noble. As the American writer Timothy White observed:

> An Amharic aristocrat, endowed with vast, untaxed lands handed down from his ancestors and augmented with gifts from the emperor, should be able to impose . . . strict standards of administration for his properties, and to employ his soldiers (Makonnen had more than six thousand men in his private army) to protect his holdings and collect rent and taxes. The privileged must be vigilant in maintaining a social order based on loyalty and humble submission on the part of their inferiors, while showing the same respect and fealty to the imperial court.

The learning of church dogma and history was perhaps the most important part of Tafari's education. He learned about the *abuna*, or chief bishop of Ethiopia, always an Egyptian appointed by the

My father had a strong desire to see the people get accustomed to the work of civilization which he had observed in Europe.
—HAILE SELASSIE

patriarch of the Coptic Church in Alexandria, Egypt. The abuna was the spiritual leader of Ethiopia's Christian establishment, from St. George's Cathedral in Addis Ababa to the tiny churches in every Christian village, more than 10,000 churches and monasteries in all. In addition to the books of the Bible recognized in Europe and the West, Tafari studied those books accepted as part of the Ethiopian version of the Holy Scriptures, such as the Book of Light, the Sixth and Seventh Books of Moses, the Ascension of Isaiah, the Books of Eden, and the Shepherd of Hermas. He also learned the *Kebra Nagast*, or Glory of the Kings, the sacred book written in the 14th century that recounts the story of the Queen of Sheba's trip to Jerusalem to visit King Solomon and of the birth of their son, Menilek, who became the first king of Ethiopia. The current emperor, whose real name was Sahala Mariam, had taken the name Menilek II in honor of the son of King Solomon and the Queen of Sheba.

In 1900 the eight-year-old student completed this part of his formal learning and was accordingly ordained as a deacon by Abuna Yohannes. In the meantime, Tafari had continued his education in the French language under Jarosseau. When he was 11, Tafari came under the guidance of a new teacher, Abba Samuel Wolde Kahen, an Ethiopian convert to Roman Catholicism, who like Jarosseau became a trusted adviser. Tafari's education in the French language and his constant encounters with Europeans gave him a crucial advantage over other young nobles from the highest ranks of the aristocracy, who were not expected to learn foreign languages or customs. That kind of training was usually reserved for the lower nobility (those with no potential claim on the throne), so that they could act as intermediaries between the emperor's court and foreign diplomats and merchants.

The care taken by Ras Makonnen for his son's education and upbringing had helped mold Tafari into an intelligent and promising young teenager. In 1905, Makonnen, impressed with his son's progress, decided it was time to give him his first taste of power.

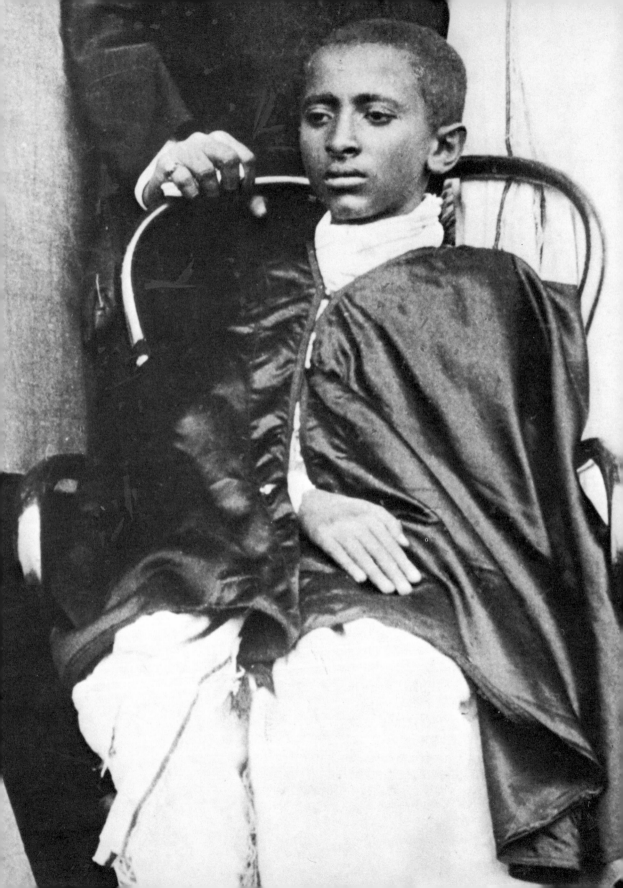

3

The Young Master of Intrigue

Tafari's political career officially began at the age of 13, on November 1, 1905, when his father bestowed on him the title of *dejazmatch* (literally "commander of the gate"), or count, and made him governor of the Gara Muletta region of Harer province.

The appointment was given for the sake of rank only; the actual administration of the region was to be performed by an appointed deputy. But it did officially mark Tafari's passage from childhood to adulthood, signifying that he was now old enough to lead his own life and build his own military and political base. To ensure that everybody took his son's appointment seriously, Ras Makonnen performed the ceremony with full pomp and rigor.

The ceremony took place on the grounds of Ras Makonnen's ghibbi outside the walls of Harer. With Tafari seated alongside his father, the proclamation announcing the appointment was read to Makonnen's army, which stood in strict ranks before them.

Tafari . . . believed that his father . . . had shown trust in him by appointing him . . . Dejazmatch of a large region of Harar Province.
—PETER SCHWAB
American historian

A 1908 portrait of 16-year-old Tafari Makonnen. Even as a teenager, Tafari showed uncommon instinctive skill at political manipulation, and by the time he was 17, many thought he would make a bid to usurp the throne.

Tafari was given a separate household with a full complement of military officers, soldiers, and servants. As Makonnen made clear to all assembled, the newly assigned men were directly under Tafari's orders and their loyalty was to be given exclusively to their new lord. Those remaining in Makonnen's army solemnly promised to transfer their obedience to the young dejazmatch in case anything happened to the ras. The ceremony ended with the traditional *gebber*, a feast that featured, for the common soldiers and for Makonnen, Tafari, and the guests of high rank, the raw meat of freshly slaughtered oxen, *injera*, (flat, moist bread) and hotly spiced *wat* (stew) of chicken or beef. *Talla* and *tedj*, strong beer and honey wine, were passed around to everyone.

Ethiopia's lone link to the outside world, the Addis Ababa–Djibouti railway that passed through Harer, now brought foreigners to Tafari's court. From audiences with the visiting foreigners, the young dejazmatch learned about politics in the rest of the world. Europeans who met Tafari at this time were impressed by his quiet attentiveness, which would prove to be a hallmark throughout his long life.

A prosperous Amhara couple eating a typical Ethiopian meal outside their tukal in a village in Shewa province. During Tafari's youth the Ethiopian nobility owned most of the nation's land, controlled private armies, and were entitled to large amounts of the peasants' labor. Peasants were also taxed by the nobility and church.

In January 1906, the 52-year-old Makonnen was stricken with typhoid and taken to the holy town of Kulubi, near Harer. His illness worsened, and by March it became clear that he would die. The American historian Harold G. Marcus, drawing from the diaries of Jarosseau, describes what happened next:

> On 20 March, the dying man entrusted all his financial papers to the British consul, admonishing him to "guard them well, and give them to my son when things have returned to normal." A little later, he worried, "Oh, if only I could have lived for a few years more, until the time when he would be able to stand up for his own rights." In order to ensure the boy a few more years of protection, Makonnen wrote Menilek, consigning Tafari to his care, mentioning that in the next life he would ask how he had acquitted the charge.
>
> When Tafari was finally summoned to his father's bedside, the ras was too weak to talk but managed to place his hand in benediction on the shoulder of the kneeling youth. He motioned Tafari to sit nearby, where the boy spent the night, a witness to the pain and suffering of his father's passing on 21 March. . . . Just before dawn the next day, Makonnen's death was announced by cannon and rifle fire, trumpets, and ululations.

It was a devastating loss for Tafari, not just because of his grief at losing his father, but also because it left him dangerously exposed politically in the cutthroat world of court politics at such an early age.

Passengers boarding the Addis Ababa–Djibouti train, Ethiopia's only form of modern transportation until the 1930s. The train passed through Harer province on its way to the French colony of Djibouti on the Red Sea, bringing Tafari into contact with Europeans who stopped at his father's court.

It did not take long for Tafari to see what his father's absence could mean at the court of the emperor. Menilek, as soon as he had heard about the death of his cousin and loyal duke, summoned Tafari and his officers to Addis Ababa for an official mourning ceremony. The young dejazmatch and his entourage left Harer on April 10 and arrived at the capital 16 days later, expecting a brief stay that would feature Tafari's appointment to take over his late father's post as governor of Harer. But to their surprise, they learned that Tafari's older half-brother, Dejazmatch Yilma, was given the job. Yilma — who was married to the niece of Empress Taitu, Menilek's wife — had better family connections than Tafari. But more important, as Menilek told the 14-year-old Tafari, he was simply too young to be entrusted with the task of running such a strategically important province. Instead, Menilek gave him control of a portion of Shewa province called Selale, a much smaller and less significant region than anything in Harer. He was not granted permission to rule Selale in person.

Tafari did not fully believe Menilek's explanation for denying him Harer. As he revealed years later in a passing remark in his autobiography, Tafari considered himself the victim of a conspiracy by Empress Taitu, who was known to promote the interests of her close relatives at the expense of others. Tafari must have been bitterly disappointed as he stood in the throne room and heard Menilek's decision, but as custom dictated, he had to bow to the emperor, express his humblest gratitude, and bow again as he left the chamber. Tafari bided his time at the emperor's court, soaking up more knowledge of court politics, and at the Menilek II School, Ethiopia's first European-style educational institution.

But then, quite suddenly, Dejazmatch Yilma died of pneumonia, after having governed Harer for only a year and a half. The governorship of the province was vacant again. Tafari's hopes rose once more, but once more they were crushed when Menilek appointed an experienced general, Dejazmatch Balcha, to govern Harer. The emperor consoled Tafari by granting portions of the large southern province of Sidamo.

This time Tafari, barely 16 years old, was allowed to rule his lands in person. Accompanied by General Abayneh, Imru, and 3,000 of his father's soldiers, he left for Sidamo on April 4, 1908, to govern a region for the first time. As governor, Tafari would be the agent of the emperor, required to put his army at Menilek's service whenever it was requested. But he would have the power to tax the population and collect other tribute for the sustenance of his army, and he was also empowered to give military and administrative positions to those under him.

Tafari spent about eight months governing his region in Sidamo, so he had little chance to make a name for himself in the position. His tenure was cut short by the political situation in Addis Ababa: Menilek had suffered a stroke, and Tafari, like all the other nobles of the empire, returned to the capital. Protocol and tradition required that they show respect by being with the emperor during his illness. But more important to all the nobles was their need, should the emperor die, to be in position for the scramble for power that would surely follow.

Tafari with Emperor Menilek in 1906, soon after Tafari's father, Ras Makonnen, died. Menilek brought Tafari to the imperial court after the dying Makonnen had asked him to look after his son. At this point Tafari was a *dejazmatch*, or count, nominally in charge of a small region within Harer province.

Menilek's wife, Empress Taitu. A strong woman who had taken part in the Battle of Adwa, Taitu used her influence with the emperor to gain promotions for her relatives. Tafari blamed her when the emperor failed to appoint him to his late father's post as governor of Harer.

Menilek was not just another in the long line of monarchs to have ruled in Ethiopia. He had expanded the nation almost to its present geographic boundaries, and he had put the country under centralized authority for the first time in centuries, stopping the constant warring between kings, dukes, and counts in the process. Indeed, the two achievements were closely related. Because of the success of Menilek's expansion to the south, there was far more land to distribute among the nobles; they no longer had to fight each other to gain control of territory. The new way to acquire territory was to win the political infighting within Menilek's court.

With the possibility of Menilek's death, the level of intrigue increased to greater heights — particularly because the emperor had no male heir. If the throne were to become vacant, a number of powerful neguses, rases, and dejazmatches, all of whom had large private armies at their disposal, could claim legitimate descent from some previous emperor. The struggle for the throne would almost certainly lead to open warfare, turning the clock back to the periods of civil war that had so devastated the country in previous times.

For Tafari, Menilek's illness was especially disconcerting. After the death of his father, the only person he could rely on to enhance his political future was the emperor himself. If Menilek were to die before Tafari could establish his own political power base, it could indeed be fatal for the young dejazmatch. As he and his retinue returned to Addis Ababa at the end of 1908, they found that nobles from the farthest corners of the empire had already arrived, or would arrive shortly. The scramble for power was on.

The 64-year-old emperor's stroke had left him incapacitated, and his condition, complicated by syphilis, was deteriorating further. It was becoming apparent to the nobles at court that he would never be able to resume effective leadership. Empress Taitu, the person Tafari felt was responsible for the disappointments in his political career, was running the country in the name of her husband. Taitu was a very strong woman with considerable influence over her husband, and she had already gained a reputation for promoting her own relatives whenever possible. She knew they would be her only protectors after the death of Menilek.

One of the last photos of Emperor Menilek, taken in 1912 at a meeting with a French representative. Tafari stands to the left and rear of the emperor, who was felled by a stroke and syphilis in 1909; Taitu ran the empire in place of her stricken husband.

As Taitu's power increased and her husband's illness left her the effective ruler of Ethiopia, she and the leading nobles clashed over who would succeed the emperor. Soon, Menilek made his decision: Tafari's cousin, Iyasu Mikael, the 13-year-old son of the powerful Ras Mikael of Welo province. *Lij* (the title for a young nobleman) Iyasu was not related to the empress, but she knew that this time there was very little she could do to alter her husband's decision. However, the empress wasted no time shoring up her position. She arranged the ceremonial marriage of Lij Iyasu to her six-year-old great-niece. Shortly thereafter, on October 30, 1909, it was publicly announced that Iyasu would be Emperor Menilek's successor. Because Lij Iyasu was too young to do the actual ruling of the empire, a regent, Ras Tesemma Nado, was selected to make all the major decisions in his stead.

While she was maneuvering the marriage between the heir to the throne and her great-niece, Taitu successfully managed to defuse a plot to strip her of power. Tafari's conduct during this extremely treacherous period was remarkably shrewd, especially for a 17-year-old. He maintained a strict neutrality, despite his belief that Taitu had been responsible for keeping him from the governorship

Tafari's cousin Lij Iyasu Mikael, chosen as heir to the throne in 1909 at the age of 13. Lij Iyasu was Menilek's grandson and the son of a ras who had converted from Islam, making many prominent Christian nobles uneasy about the choice. The reserved Tafari and the exuberant Iyasu briefly attended school together in Addis.

of Harer. He refused to cooperate with the plotters seeking to oust the empress, yet at the same time he refused to reveal the names of the conspirators to Taitu. Thus he proved his loyalty to the empress without betraying his integrity, winning the admiration of both sides. On March 3, 1910, Empress Taitu rewarded Tafari with what he wanted most: the governorship of Harer province.

The empress's luck finally ran out just three weeks later, when several powerful nobles and the leaders of the Ethiopian Orthodox Church moved against her. Claiming that she was undermining Lij Iyasu's and Ras Tesemma's rightful authority, they relieved her of all administrative duties. Her sole job, they informed her in no uncertain terms, was to take care of her sick husband.

The conspirators who deposed the empress nullified all the promotions she had made since the onset of Menilek's illness, except for one: that of Dejazmatch Tafari, who would continue as governor of Harer. Tafari seemed to have won a very important political victory. He had gotten back his father's governorship without antagonizing any political bloc, and he had gained the respect of all groups for being loyal and principled.

But before he left for Harer, the regent, Ras Tesemma, wanted assurances that Tafari's ambition for the throne would be kept in check. To make certain that Tafari would not challenge Lij Iyasu's claim to the throne, the regent asked Tafari to take an oath administered by Abuna Matewos, now the leader of the Ethiopian church.

According to Haile Selassie's autobiography, the oath specified that upon Menilek's death Tafari would not seek Lij Iyasu's throne, nor would Tafari's officers advise him to do so. As part of the same oath, Lij Iyasu and Ras Tesemma swore not to remove Tafari from the governorship of Harer.

His new post secured, Tafari took leave from all the nobles — and, ever sensitive to protocol, the now powerless empress — and left for Harer. He was about to take command of a powerful army and a large, important province. And he was regarded by all as a serious threat to seize the throne.

Abuna (Bishop) Matewos, head of the Ethiopian Orthodox Church. Matewos, like all previous abunas, was an Egyptian named to the post by the patriarch of Alexandria. After Tafari was appointed governor of Harer and thus became a threat to seize the throne, Matewos made him and Lij Iyasu swear an oath of loyalty to each other.

4

The Path to the Throne

Tafari arrived in the city of Harer with a free hand to administer Harer province as he saw fit. Harer was a fortress and market town built to control the ancient caravan routes between the fertile lands to the north, the desert to the south, and the sea to the east. It had been an independent Muslim city-state for centuries, until it was conquered by the Egyptians in the 1870s. After Menilek's 1887 conquest of the town and the surrounding region, Christian Ethiopians were sent to Harer as administrators and settlers, but they were still greatly outnumbered by the Muslim population.

Harer's narrow, winding streets were lined with old, crumbling houses, brothels and tedj bars, and stores run by Greeks, Armenians, and Indians. Minarets rose above the jumble of buildings, marking the mosques of the city's Muslim majority, made up of Hareris, Somalis, Oromos, and Arabs. By day the town teemed with activity, with traders bringing camels laden with goods to merchants, and buyers and sellers arguing over prices in a variety of different languages. Outside the city's three jails, the families of prisoners lined up to feed their relatives, who were kept in chains.

Tafari went to Harar in 1910 and proceeded to build a personal following loyal to him.
—PETER SCHWAB
American historian

Tafari in 1928, after he had been named *negus*, or king (the *1921* that appears below his signature was the year according to the Ethiopian calendar, which runs seven years behind the Western calendar). By this time Tafari, already running the government, had captured the imagination of the foreign press.

After sunset, when the gates in the city walls were shut, hyenas prowled the empty streets, disturbed only by the occasional pedestrian carrying a rifle or pistol to protect himself against robbers. Outside the walls stood the round huts of a large leper colony and the ghibbi built by Ras Makonnen.

Tafari, now the commander of his father's large army, settled in at Makonnen's ghibbi. Upon conquering Harer, Menelik had taken two-thirds of the province's lands from the Muslim population and given it to his Ethiopian warlords and soldiers; now, 23 years later, the Ethiopian Christian minority that still controlled Harer lived in fear of an uprising by a resentful native population. Tafari's task was to appease the Muslim peasants while preserving the privileges of the Christian ruling class. His father, the province's first governor, had done so without resorting to military terrorization of the general population. But the next two governors, Yilma and Balcha, often used their armies to keep the people of Harer in submission.

A 1950 photo of the ancient walled city of Harer, where Tafari arrived in 1910 to govern Harer province. The predominantly Muslim province had been ruled harshly by the two previous Amhara governors, but Tafari cut taxes and instituted a legal system. The modest reforms did not threaten the dominance of the province's Christian nobility.

Tafari chose to rule with a lighter hand than Yilma and Balcha, who had raised taxes greatly during their governorships. Tafari cut the tax rate in half, back down to the level originally set by Makonnen. The young dejazmatch reduced the power of the province's local lords, limiting their right to demand work from the peasants, and created a system of courts to extend legal rights to the peasantry. Tafari's reforms, though resented by many Christian nobles and settlers, were welcomed by the province's Muslim majority. Still, they were not fundamental reforms, merely moderate measures that preserved the status quo — a preview of how Tafari would rule the nation once he became emperor.

Ras Tesemma died on April 10, 1911, not long after Tafari had arrived in Harer, but his death had little effect on the 19-year-old dejazmatch. Both he and Lij Iyasu continued to honor the oath Ras Tesemma and Abuna Matewos had bound them to. Iyasu even offered his niece's hand in marriage, and Tafari accepted. The woman was Woizero Menen Asfaw, the 22-year-old granddaughter of Ras Mikael and a member of an aristocratic family in Welo province. Tafari and Menen were married in a church ceremony on July 31, 1911. The marriage would last till the death of Empress Menen in 1961, and together they would have 6 children (Tafari had already fathered an illegitimate daughter by another woman when he was 17). Tafari was happy in his relationship with his wife, a woman of "goodness," as he described her with characteristic reserve in his autobiography.

As Tafari and Menen settled into married life in Harer, many at the great ghibbi in Addis Ababa were becoming disgruntled with the crown prince. Lij Iyasu was an intelligent teenager, and those in favor of modernization had high hopes for him. His contact with groups outside the traditional Amhara-Tigrean ruling circles, unusual for a noble, showed a keen intellect and led one European diplomat to say of Iyasu, "when he becomes Emperor . . . he will astonish everyone by his intelligence and system of government, which would be carried out according to some European criteria and with justice, especially for the Galla [Muslim] population." However,

Menen Asfaw at the age of 22, just prior to her July 1911 wedding to Tafari. Their marriage would last 50 years, until her death in 1961. During the power struggle between Tafari and Lij Iyasu, Menen, who was Iyasu's niece, stayed in the background.

Lij Iyasu, the crown prince, shortly after the death of Menilek in December 1913. Although at 17 too young to formally become emperor, he tried to initiate a number of reforms designed to end discrimination against Ethiopia's large Muslim population. He traveled to Harer and overruled Tafari on several occasions.

it was these very characteristics — coupled with his relentless womanizing, which many nobles considered undignified — that brought to bear a host of powerful forces against his reign. His worst offense, in the eyes of many among the Christian nobility, was his father's Muslim upbringing (Ras Mikael's original name had been Mohammed Ali), leading them to suspect Iyasu of holding pro-Muslim sympathies himself.

Emperor Menilek finally died on December 12, 1913. His body was buried quickly, without announcement or ceremony, and his wife Taitu was moved secretly with a small retinue to a nearby monastery. Although Iyasu was not yet 18, the age at which he would have the right to ascend the throne, he now had the power to make the important decisions of state. His seal replaced that of Menilek, and he became the chairman of the regent's council, the official ruling body of the country.

On May 31, 1914, Iyasu named his father, Mikael, negus and extended his dominions beyond Welo to include the entire province of Tigre. The move angered the Tigrean nobles, some of whom were so incensed that they led their forces against Negus Mikael's army. A large battle ensued, and peace was restored only after Mikael named one of the Tigrean aristocrats a ras and appointed him to govern Tigre, offering his daughter's hand in marriage for good measure. But the resentment against Iyasu remained; his overthrow became a subject of open discussion among many leading nobles in the capital.

Some European diplomats in Addis Ababa were also dissatisfied with Iyasu, but for different reasons. The start of World War I in Europe and the early successes of the German and Turkish forces against those of France and Britain concerned the representatives of the latter two nations in Addis Ababa. They were worried that Iyasu's Muslim background might lead him to ally with the Turks, who they feared would incite uprisings among the Muslim populations in many French and British colonies in Africa and the Middle East. Some Europeans and Ethiopians speculated that Iyasu had actually converted to Islam. Whether that was true or whether he was just trying to end Ethiopia's historic discrimination against its Muslim population is a subject not yet settled among historians.

But the American historian Harold G. Marcus points out that Lij Iyasu's efforts to improve the lot of the empire's Muslims led him to directly interfere with Tafari's rule over Harer. Iyasu made several trips to Harer, appointed Muslims to high official posts and to serve as policemen, imposed a tax on the Christian nobility, and made frequent visits to the central mosque. Ethiopians who were present report that the crown prince told Muslim leaders, "through we differ in religion and tribe, I would wish all of us to be united through a nationalist sentiment." Iyasu's reforms were going much further than Tafari's, and the Christian nobility was outraged.

In June 1915, Tafari received a blow of another kind: He almost died when a boat he and nine of his aides were in sank during an outing on a lake near Harer. Seven drowned, including Tafari's long-time teacher and faithful adviser, Abba Samuel, who sacrificed his own life to save the young lord. As Tafari later wrote, using the royal "our" in referring to himself: "our soul had been barely prevented from getting separated from our body."

While Tafari recovered from his harrowing experience, Lij Iyasu's anticolonial sentiments had become obvious. In October 1915, he angered the British legation by sending an eight-camel caravan, laden with ammunition, to Sayyid Mohammed bin Abdullah, the Somali leader who had mobilized his people against the British colonial government in British Somaliland. The British had been informed of the shipment by Tafari, through whose province the caravan passed. Cleverly, yet without violating the terms of the oath he had taken with Ras Tesemma and Lij Iyasu, Tafari was getting back at the crown prince for overruling his authority in Harer —and chipping away at Iyasu's hold on the throne.

Lij Iyasu, meanwhile, was compounding the damage to his own position in many ways. For example, on April 27, 1916, at a reception celebrating the birthday of the sultan of Turkey, the crown prince committed an enormous faux pas. Iyasu supposedly

One of Tafari's servants, an Oromo. Ethiopia's Muslim Oromos, as well as the rest of the empire's Muslims (amounting to 40 percent of the total population), were forbidden to own land. Iyasu's pro-Muslim efforts led to a coup and brief civil war initiated by Christian nobles that resulted in Iyasu's ouster.

gave the Turkish ambassador an Ethiopian flag embroidered with the Islamic slogan, "God is great and Mohammed is his prophet." Although Iyasu later told the British ambassador that one of his aides had made the flag and that the aide had since been put in chains, the incident reinforced the belief that Iyasu had abandoned Christianity for Islam.

Soon several important Ethiopian church officials in the capital, as well as the many nobles who had been removed from their posts by Iyasu over the previous three years, were actively working with British and French diplomats for the overthrow of the crown prince. Tafari returned to Addis Ababa to be close to the situation, and very possibly to take part in the plotting. Publicly he kept his distance from the conspiracy while at the same time showing no strong commitment to Iyasu's leadership.

Iyasu's men reported that the dejazmatch was in on the conspiracy. Iyasu forbade Tafari from returning to Harer and instead left for Harer himself, leaving behind some of his soldiers to watch Tafari in case he tried to leave Addis Ababa. When Iyasu reached Dire Dawa, a town close to the city of Harer city, he sent word that he had stripped Tafari of the governorship of Harer; Iyasu would now rule the province, and Tafari would take over the less prestigious governorship of Kefa. Iyasu also ordered Menen to join her husband in Addis Ababa immediately and continue on to Kefa with him. She was to bring her two-year-old daughter, Tenegne Worq, and her two-month-old son, Asfa Wossen, the first two children Tafari and Menen had had together.

Now Tafari openly joined the conspiracy against Iyasu; the oath that he and his cousin had sworn under Ras Tesemma no longer mattered. Shortly thereafter in Addis Ababa, on the morning of September 27, 1916, charges accusing Lij Iyasu of converting to Islam and aiding Turkey and Germany were read out in front of the assembled nobles and Abuna Matewos. The nobles asked the abuna to excommunicate the crown prince, but he refused, saying that there was insufficient evidence for such an action. After a heated dispute the meeting dispersed, but a small group of the foremost nobles — which probably included Tafari—remained behind.

The following day a dramatic proclamation was issued: Lij Iyasu was overthrown. For the first time since the legendary Queen of Sheba, an empress would rule Ethiopia: the 40-year-old Zawditu, Menilek's daughter. Her policies would be implemented by a new regent, Tafari Makonnen, who was named a ras. And then came the most dramatic announcement of all: Tafari would be the first regent in Ethiopian history to be heir to the throne.

Tafari's appointment to this post was a compromise solution to keep the balance between the forces of modernization and the forces of tradition. The more conservative nobility were generally fearful of some of the progressive ideas and practices Tafari had implemented during his governorship of Harer. Other nobles believed that some modernization was needed to deal with the Europeans, who were becoming increasingly important to Ethiopia. By putting the more traditional Zawditu on the throne, the nobles retained the option to oust Ras Tafari if he proved too radical.

Empress Zawditu (seated), Menilek's daughter, was chosen by the nobles to replace the overthrown Iyasu in September 1916. Tafari (left), who had discreetly taken part in the coup, was named a ras, heir to the throne, and regent, which made him head of government. At first relatively powerless, he soon built a strong power base.

A 1917 portrait of Ras Tafari holding binoculars, symbol of his belief in modernization. After nearly dying in the influenza epidemic of 1918, Tafari began his modernization program, bringing electricity, printing presses, and motorcars to the capital. He also established the empire's first law courts.

52

Chaos broke out as soon as word of the announcement spread. In Harer, Iyasu's forces deserted and left Dejazmatch Balcha's army unopposed as it entered the city on October 9 and massacred hundreds of Muslim civilians. Meanwhile in the northeast, Negus Mikael marched on the capital with 30,000 soldiers to avenge his son's overthrow. On October 17, Mikael's forces destroyed the army of Ras Lul Seged, who was killed in the fighting. But instead of closing in on Addis Ababa Mikael's army looted the countryside, allowing the new regime's forces to dig in opposite them. On October 27, at Segele, the battle was joined; it was the first one that Tafari ever participated in. Some 7,000 of Negus Mikael's soldiers and 3,000 soldiers of the new regime were killed before Mikael was captured and imprisoned.

Lij Iyasu was the next to challenge the new goverment. He made his way to his home province of Welo and raised an army, which for the next several months joined with the province's peasant population to harass government forces. But Iyasu's army was finally defeated on August 27, 1917, and he escaped with a few supporters while the new regime's troops pillaged the province. The deposed crown prince was finally captured in 1921 and imprisoned near Harer. There, according to stories that later circulated among foreigners, Lij Iyasu was kept manacled in specially forged chains of gold, and the monotony of his imprisonment was relieved by the affections of the beautiful women Tafari regularly sent to his cell.

Though the warfare was over and Ras Tafari was fully installed as regent, he was not yet firmly in charge of the government. The real power belonged to the council of ministers, which was controlled by older, conservative nobles who had risen to their overlordships under Menilek. British and Italian diplomats thought at the time that the frail young ras would prove no match for the experienced conservatives, but they were quickly proven wrong. Tafari tirelessly built up his power base by quietly distributing money to the citizens and soldiers of Addis Ababa, thus earning their support. It paid off in March 1918, when a large crowd of angry demonstrators led by army officers demanded the resignations of the council of ministers. Zawditu gave in and fired the ministers, which left Tafari a free hand to consolidate his own power.

Tafari began to appoint his own men to fill key posts and create an elite loyal to him. But his efforts were abruptly stopped by another brush with death. The influenza epidemic that swept the world in 1918 reached Ethiopia in August of that year, and Tafari was one of the first to fall ill. A week later his condition had deteriorated so badly that the abuna gave him the last rites, but he rallied and recovered — "spared from death," as he later put it, "by God's greatness." He was among the lucky ones; by December, about 10,000 of Addis Ababa's 50,000 residents had died of the disease, including several nobles and key members of the government. Thousands fled, leaving bodies lying in the streets of the nearly deserted capital.

After the epidemic ended in 1919, Ras Tafari renewed his push for reform. He started to create a modern, centralized bureaucracy by giving each government ministry a separate office and a European adviser. In 1921, regular courts of law were established, a first for Ethiopia. The nation's first two printing presses were in operation in 1922; soon the first Amharic newspaper, a weekly, was being distributed. Motorcars and electric generators were brought to the capital, and telephone and telegraph service was expanded. Tafari outlawed the inhumane treatment of prisoners, brutal methods of execution, and other practices he considered cruel. Years later, a former Ethiopian court official told the Polish journalist Ryszard Kapuściński:

> He abolished by decree a method we call *lebasha*, for the discovery of thieves. Medicine men would give a secret herb to small boys, who, dizzy, stupefied, and directed by supernatural forces, would go into a house and point out the thief. The one who had been pointed out, in accordance with tradition, had his hands and legs cut off. Just try to imagine, my friend, life in a country where, even though you are completely innocent of crime, you can at any moment have your hands and legs cut off. . . . Only when you imagine such a life can

> *[Tafari] moved with incredible speed to gain the upper hand over Zauditu and to rally all the forces that he could muster against her.*
> —PETER SCHWAB
> American historian

53

Two high churchmen at the Ethiopian monastery in Jerusalem, the first stop on Tafari's 1924 state journey. Tafari was the highest-ranking Ethiopian ever to travel abroad. His encounters with European kings and prime ministers were widely covered by the European and North American press.

you understand the profundity of the breakthroughs that His Distinguished Highness made.

Convinced that Ethiopia's sovereignty could only be secured by strengthening the nation's hand in international diplomacy, Tafari successfully petitioned for Ethiopia's acceptance into the League of Nations in 1923. He encouraged the forging of commercial links with Europe, which dramatically increased the nation's revenue. The nobles profited, though none more than Ras Tafari himself. As Harold G. Marcus noted, the regent not only participated personally in all the commercial ventures that the state granted to foreigners, he even directed his newly appointed loyalists in the treasury to collect a personal tax on each sack of grain, cereals, and salt exported or imported.

Such activities were not considered corrupt. For centuries, Ethiopia's nobility and peasantry alike believed that the nobles owned the nation and were therefore entitled to most of the money Ethiopia could generate. The nobles had amassed fortunes for themselves for generations by pocketing the taxes they had collected from the peasants; now, with the advent of foreign trade, Tafari and the nobles enriched themselves to a far greater extent. It was, after all, much easier to tax imports and exports than the millions of poor peasant farmers working small plots of land.

Ras Tafari spent some of his newfound fortune by financing several charities and bankrolling the education abroad of a number of the empire's promising young students — thus guaranteeing the support of a new generation of Ethiopians. To further safeguard his position, he also doled out large amounts to buy the loyalty of the military. Some foreign observers were appalled by Ras Tafari's constant use of the state coffers for his own purposes. The French ambassador to Ethiopia said that Tafari was "venal and corrupt," calling him "a grasping man" who took every opportunity "to acquire, whether at the expense of the people's interest or the Treasury, a personal fortune."

Seeking a treaty from either France, Italy, or Britain that would give Ethiopia a port on the Red Sea, Tafari embarked on his first trip outside the country on April 16, 1924. Accompanied by a large entourage, he left Addis Ababa for French-controlled Djibouti, and from there he and his party left by steamship for Palestine on the way to stops in Jerusalem and Cairo. From there it was on to France, and when the 32-year-old ras arrived at the French port of Marseilles, Tafari had finally realized his lifelong dream of seeing Europe.

The first European leader he met was the president of France, Alexandre Millerand, who accorded the regent full honors befitting the representative of a free African nation. Next, Tafari was received with magnificent hospitality by the king of Italy, Victor Emmanuel III, and by Italy's prime minister, Benito Mussolini — ironically, the man who would order the invasion of Ethiopia 11 years later. Tafari was also given warm welcomes in Sweden and Greece, but in London he was snubbed by the British king and government officials. Nevertheless, the British newspapers were supportive of the exotic Ethiopian ras. The *Times* of London applauded his modernization policies and his travels abroad, saying, "the tremendous rupture with the past which this journey . . . involves shows the boldness, the resolution, and the enlightenment of the prince's character."

Tafari's tour failed to secure an outlet to the sea for Ethiopia; neither the French, the Italians, nor the British, all of whom had colonies adjacent to Ethiopia on the Red Sea, would agree to Tafari's request to negotiate an agreement under which Ethiopia would gain a port. But his trip was a huge personal success. The Western press was fascinated by Tafari, by the independent African kingdom he represented, and by the six lions and four zebras he brought with him to present as gifts to European heads of state.

Newspaper stories describing the trip were picked up in the United States and in the Caribbean, capturing the imaginations of blacks in those places at

French officers conduct Ras Tafari on a tour of the Paris airport during his 1924 trip. Newspaper accounts of his meetings with European heads of state were greeted with pride by U.S. and Caribbean blacks, who regarded Tafari's African kingdom as a glowing example of black independence.

a time when they were rediscovering their African heritage. Jamaicans especially took notice of Tafari; in 1916, the Jamaican black nationalist leader Marcus Garvey reportedly gave a speech in which he told listeners to "look to Africa for the crowning of a black king; he shall be the Redeemer." The impoverished blacks of Jamaica saw that Ras Tafari, the heir to the Ethiopian throne, might become that king. It was the prophecy that led to the Jamaican religion known as Rastafarianism.

But that was still several years in the future. Tafari returned from Europe to face a disgruntled aristocracy in Addis Ababa. Zawditu and her supporters considered Tafari's trip another attempt at self-glorification. The lower nobility, meanwhile, felt that the empire was now paying too much attention to international trade, rather than taxing the peasantry, which was still their main source of income. The resentment led to a plot to assassinate Tafari, but it was uncovered and the nobles accused of instigating it were jailed.

Tafari continued to build his political base at the capital, putting more of his own people in key positions. By the end of 1926, with the death of Abuna Matewos and other members of Menilek's old guard, the conservatives were quickly losing ground. Meanwhile Tafari gained new allies among the large segment of nobles who were benefiting from the growing foreign trade, which by now included India, the United States, and most countries in Europe.

The new modernization also meant greater centralization than ever before. Increasingly, the bulk of the state's revenue was coming from foreign trade rather than tribute from peasants. The central government began exercising tight fiscal control over the provinces, thus undermining the traditional authority of provincial leaders. This created hostility toward Tafari from such powerful local lords as Balcha (now a ras), who came to the capital escorted by 5,000 troops to pressure the regent in February 1928. His attempt to muster some support from Empress Zawditu against Tafari failed when the cunning regent ordered 2,000 policemen to surround Ras Balcha's forces, who dispersed without firing a shot. After a brief imprisonment, Balcha was forced into retirement.

Tafari decided that the time had come to take the biggest prize of all. In September 1928, Tafari told his supporters to demand that the empress name him negus and remove her people from the palace. Zawditu, with few supporters left, had little choice but to agree. On September 22 she made Tafari a king.

The official ceremony took place on October 7, 1928. The only thing now standing between "His Majesty King Tafari Makonnen, heir to the throne of Ethiopia and Regent Plenipotentiary" and the imperial scepter was the existence of Empress Zawditu.

5

The Emperor

Tafari awaited the right moment to deliver the final stroke that would give him the throne, and it wasn't long before the moment arrived. In 1928 northern Ethiopia was hit by drought and locusts, and by early 1929 a famine had struck the region. Insensitive to the plight of the impoverished peasants, provincial lords continued to insist on tax payments. The peasants revolted.

Tafari ordered Ras Gugsa Wolie, the governor of the northern province of Gonder, to use his army to put down the revolt. At first the choice of Gugsa seemed odd; a former husband of Empress Zawditu, he was known to resent Tafari's treatment of the empress. But the negus knew what was coming. When Gugsa joined the rebels and moved to lead a combined attack on the capital, Tafari was already prepared. His army, led by Ras Mulugeta, met Ras Gugsa's army on March 31, 1930, near Debre Tabor.

Uneasy lies the head that wears the crown.
—ancient proverb

Tafari wearing the emperor's crown in 1930, when he became Haile Selassie I, King of the Kings of Ethiopia. He seized the throne in April 1930 after his forces defeated the army of a rebel ras, who was killed in the fighting. Two days later Empress Zawditu died mysteriously, making Tafari the new emperor.

The battle was over quickly. Tafari had a secret weapon: the Imperial Air Force. Although the air force consisted of only one plane, piloted by a Frenchman, it was the first time in Ethiopian history that an airplane had been used in battle. Ras Gugsa's 10,000-man army, terrified upon seeing what they considered "God's punishment from the skies," fled in panic. In less than three hours the battle was over; Gugsa was among those killed.

The rout of Ras Gugsa was a stark demonstration that Tafari's forces, which by now could be called the forces of the central government, were far too strong for the traditional armies of the provincial warlords. Furthermore, it showed those nobles who might be considering the overthrow of Tafari that he was able to defeat a large provincial army without actually being present on the battlefield himself — a marked departure from the age-old tradition of a noble accompanying his men in warfare. In the past, an Ethiopian noble could hope to kill a rival noble in battle; such an event would end the battle instantly. But if Negus Tafari was not going to be present during the fighting, there was no way to get to him.

Just two days after the death of her former husband, Empress Zawditu died under mysterious circumstances. The official explanation was that she had succumbed to paratyphoid fever and diabetes, but many suspected that Tafari had had her poisoned. The next evening, after a hurried funeral ceremony performed by the new abuna, Zawditu's body was interred in Menilek's mausoleum.

Early the following morning, the council of state unanimously named Tafari emperor of Ethiopia. For most of his 38 years, Tafari Makonnen had maneuvered quietly, flawlessly, and singlemindedly to attain the throne. Now it was his.

He chose November 2, 1930, as the date of the official coronation. He planned the coronation specifically to advertise to the rest of the world that the new emperor was a reformist who wanted to rule his country by the standards of European monarchs and thus needed to be treated as their equal. He wanted to show the developed nations that a new era in Ethiopian politics was about to begin.

The seven months between the death of Zawditu and Tafari's coronation were used to prepare Addis Ababa for the grand occasion. Though the city had existed for only 40 years, it was already the largest in the empire, boasting modern buildings, electricity, and a handful of automobiles, the only ones in the country. Yet it still resembled a traditional Amhara town. Whole sections of Addis, as it was called by Ethiopians, featured the round huts with cone-shaped roofs and dirt roads found throughout the highlands of Shewa and the northern provinces.

Construction crews, run mostly by Armenian contractors whose families had lived in Ethiopia in some cases for generations, worked to give the city a more modern look in time for the arrival of the foreign press and high-ranking European dignitaries. Houses and buildings along the major streets were repaired, and electric lights were installed to light the route. High walls were erected to hide the poorest sections of Addis Ababa, and beggars were rounded up and transported to a camp outside the capital. Tafari even oversaw the design of modern uniforms and other trappings for the royal family and the Ethiopian aristocracy. The money needed for the enormously expensive coronation project was raised through extra taxes on merchants and the nobility — and, of course, on the already impoverished general public.

Addis Ababa, with the royal palace on the horizon at center right. Seven months of preparation were set aside for Tafari's coronation, which was to take place in November 1930. Buildings in the city were refurbished and electric lights were installed. Nobles and their private armies streamed in from the provinces.

Tafari on coronation day, November 2, 1930, surrounded by church officials and important nobles. He took the name Haile Selassie, Amharic for "Might of the Trinity."

As the big day approached, special trains from Djibouti brought journalists and foreign dignitaries to Addis to witness the coronation of the new emperor of Abyssinia, as Ethiopia was called by Europeans. By the end of October, delegations from throughout western and southern Europe, Egypt, Japan, and the United States had arrived; the highest-ranking foreign representative was the Duke of Gloucester, who in six years would become King George VI of Britain.

At the same time, Ethiopian churchmen and nobles streamed into the city from the farthest corners of the empire. Powerful rases and dejazmatches, dressed traditionally in capes made of lion pelts and headdresses made of peacock feathers, rode through the already crowded streets on mules, each followed on foot by a personal escort of several dozen heavily armed men. Ras Hailu of Gojam province, the most powerful provincial lord, brought his entire personal army of 25,000 men. Tafari himself presented the perfect mix of modernity and traditional splendour. As the British novelist and satirist Evelyn Waugh, in Addis to report on the coronation for the *Times* of London, wrote: "Sometimes the emperor passes in a great red car surrounded by cantering lancers. A page sits behind holding over his head an umbrella of crimson silk embroidered with sequins and gold tassels."

On the afternoon of November 1, 1930, the coronation week began with the unveiling of a statue of Menilek II in front of St. George's Cathedral. The emperor wrote in his autobiography that the moment "the statue was seen, the joy in the hearts of Ethiopians was inestimable." An interesting observation, because no Ethiopians were allowed near the ceremony. According to the British historian Christopher Clapham, "the humble Abyssinians stood off at a distance, a considerable distance, and saw what they could. Yet some of these tribesmen had walked hundreds of miles to reach Addis, coming from provinces so remote that they had been marching for weeks to get there on time."

Early the next morning, the foreign dignitaries returned to St. George's, where the coronation ceremony was to be held. The royal couple had been in the cathedral since the previous night performing a prayer vigil, accompanied by the highest officials of the Ethiopian Orthodox Church. Once the dignitaries had arrived, the church service, conducted with great solemnity, continued for another two hours. Sacred texts were chanted, choirs sang hymns, and priests swayed rythmically to the beat of drums as incense burned throughout the church.

The service ended, and Abuna Kyrillos, Negus Tafari, and Menen led the procession outside the cathedral, where Tafari was anointed with sacred oil and crowned. Now he took a new name: Haile Selassie — Amharic for "Might of the Trinity" — the 225th Emperor of the Solomonic Dynasty, Elect of God, Lord of Lords, King of Kings, Conquering Lion of the Tribes of Judah.

Next the crown prince, Asfa Wossen, was installed as heir to the throne, followed by the empress and the rest of the royal family in order of succession. Finally, Haile Selassie and his escort retired with the clergy into the cathedral for a 90-minute mass. When the royal couple reappeared, a visiting British naval band played the newly composed national anthem while the Imperial Air Force, now up to three planes, flew overhead. As the crown prince knelt facing his father in a demonstration of submission and respect, a 101-gun salute was fired.

> *Certainly, the emperor's statement that joy was seen in the hearts of all Ethiopians upon the unveiling of the statue was ludicrous, as few Ethiopians were present to see it.*
> —PETER SCHWAB
> American historian

Haile Selassie's eldest son and heir, Asfa Wossen, leads Britain's Duke of Gloucester (the future King George VI) during coronation ceremonies. The press showed up in force to record the event, which was attended by top government officials from around the world. Haile Selassie intended it to advertise Ethiopia's status as a modern state.

The royal couple then went for a two-mile drive around the city in a horse-drawn coach to show themselves to the rest of the population in the capital. Over the next few days a series of ceremonies and banquets were held, concluding with a huge military review of the empire's soldiers, all of them in traditional dress: barefoot and wearing white *shammas*, or cotton robes. On November 4 the general public's turn to view their emperor finally came when the royal couple were blessed by the ordinary clergy. The emperor and his wife proceeded from church to church, distributing alms to the poor.

Exactly as Haile Selassie had planned, accounts of the coronation made the front pages of newspapers all over the world, accompanied by photographs of foreign dignitaries paying their respects to Ethiopia's new emperor. His manner, always reserved and regal, now became even more severe to match the majesty of his title. At official banquets given by various delegations, he would appear with a slight smile on his face and sit at the center of the foremost table, stiff and unmoving throughout. As the American historian Peter Schwab wrote, "A few words now and then to dignitaries seated next to him would force him to move slightly. The emperor then, and henceforth, was always keenly aware of his demeanor. Though polite and often gracious, he usually gave the impression of being carved in rock."

The coronation ceremonies over, Haile Selassie started his modernization program in earnest. He appointed educated Ethiopians to run government ministries and fill leading posts in the provinces, and although all the appointments were given to nobles who had demonstrated their loyalty to him, the emperor also based his choices on competence and intelligence, a departure from tradition. In addition, each ministry was assigned a hired foreign adviser: There was a black American, F. E. Work, at the ministry of education, and Everett A. Colson, a white American, at the ministry of finance.

By early 1932, the government had more than a hundred Europeans and a few Americans on the payroll, serving the state in various capacities. Some of the advisers left their jobs, frustrated by the slow implementation of the reforms they had advocated. Their most frequent complaint was that the emperor introduced only those reforms that insured profits for himself.

By European standards, the rate of reform might have seemed slow, but for traditional Ethiopia it was dizzyingly fast. Haile Selassie's unrelenting centralization took the power of taxation and management of fiscal matters away from the provincial lords and gave it instead to the ministry of finance. Soon the emperor started exercising veto power over every expenditure exceeding $10 anywhere in the nation, a practice — which would have been impossible were it not for his remarkable memory — that he would continue until the end of his reign more than 40 years later.

There was one last attempt to undermine Haile Selassie's reign. In 1932, Ras Hailu successfully arranged the escape of Lij Iyasu from his luxurious imprisonment. But government troops seized Hailu before he could muster his army and take back the throne for Iyasu. The ras was condemned to life imprisonment, Iyasu was recaptured, and 20 of their associates were executed.

The emperor set up a committee of traditional nobles and educated modernizers to draft the first constitution in Ethiopia's history. The document, completed in 1931, affirmed three basic principles:

Ras Hailu — governor of Gojam province, commander of an army of 25,000, and the wealthiest man in Ethiopia — was jailed in 1932 for freeing the imprisoned Lij Iyasu in an attempt to overthrow Haile Selassie. In the late 1930s Hailu was freed and became a leader of the Ethiopian resistance against the Italian occupation.

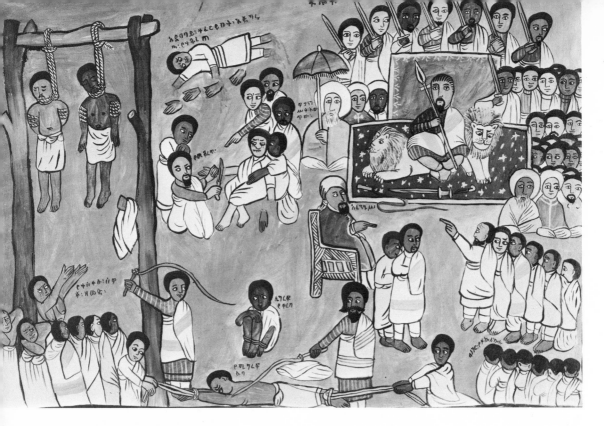

A depiction of punishments ordered in tribunal by Emperor Tewodros II, who reigned in the 1860s. Haile Selassie abolished these and other excessively cruel punishments for criminal offenses. His legal reforms included the gradual abolition of slavery, the drafting of a constitution, and the establishment of a nominal parliament.

that Ethiopia was united under one law and one emperor, that all Ethiopians were equal under the law, and that a two-chamber parliament would enable the common people to participate in government. The upper house of the parliament consisted of the emperor's hand-picked appointees, and the lower house of parliament was eventually to be elected by the public. But Haile Selassie retained the right to overrule any decision the parliament made.

The emperor enacted Ethiopia's first legal code to replace the traditional church laws that had served as the empire's legal code for centuries. He also moved to bring to an end an old Ethiopian institution — slavery. Local lords throughout the empire owned thousands of slaves; most of them were prisoners captured in wars of conquest, or their descendants. Europeans had long called for the abolition of slavery in Ethiopia (it had been an obstacle to Ethiopia's acceptance into the League of Nations in the early 1920s). Haile Selassie knew that his nation would never be considered civilized until abolition had been brought about, so in 1931 he ruled that all children born to slaves would henceforth be free. But he did not free current slaves; to have done so would have risked the wrath of the powerful lords the emperor needed on his side. The gradual abolition of slavery, which was not completed until the 1940s, was the kind of slow reform that would mark the emperor's reign.

On the economic front, Haile Selassie used $320,000 of his own money to help finance a deal to transform the Bank of Abyssinia, owned and run by the Bank of Egypt, into a national bank run entirely by Ethiopia. In other areas, a road-building program was undertaken to link the capital with all the important towns in the country. The roads were primitive and often unusable for motor vehicles, but they were the first ever built in the empire and they stimulated the growth of trade. The bids from foreign contractors and the tolls later collected on the roads brought money into the national treasury — and into the pockets of the emperor and the nobility. Education was also expanded, with more young nobles entering the Menilek II School. Several students were sent to Europe for advanced education.

But while the new emperor was pursuing his modernization program at home, Mussolini was building up Italian forces in Eritrea and Italian Somaliland, waiting for an excuse to invade Ethiopia. The Italian dictator was convinced that his overcrowded nation's chronically depressed economy would be relieved if he expanded Italy's holdings in Africa. He was obsessed with the idea that Italy, through military conquest and territorial expansion, must return to the glorious days of the Roman Empire — and he was consumed by the dream of avenging the humiliation that Italy had suffered at Adwa in 1896.

By early 1934, Mussolini was certain that the great powers in Europe, especially France and England, would not in any way defend Ethiopia as the charter of the League of Nations required. In the meantime, Mussolini's forces in Italian Somaliland had crossed the poorly delineated border and penetrated deep into the desert in the Ogaden region of Ethiopia. There they dug in around the wells at Walwal, claiming that the oasis was part of Italian Somaliland.

Victorious Italian troops carved a gigantic likeness of Mussolini into a mountainside at Adwa. The Italian dictator had long exhorted his nation to avenge the humiliating defeat suffered there in 1896. With the conquest of Ethiopia, Mussolini's dream of an Italian East African empire was attained.

Mussolini stands atop an armored vehicle to address part of the 250,000-man Italian army poised to invade Ethiopia from the Italian colony of Eritrea. Haile Selassie repeatedly asked the League of Nations to intervene during the 10 months prior to the October 1935 invasion, but to no avail.

Haile Selassie sent a force to Walwal, awaiting the arrival of a League of Nations commission to clearly define the international border separating Ethiopia from Italian Somaliland. At the end of November 1934 the commission, consisting of a group of British officials and surveyors, arrived and began its investigation while the two hostile armies, entrenched within sight of each other, looked on. At 3:00 P.M. on December 5, a whistle blew on the Italian side, followed by a barrage of gunfire. The Ethiopian forces returned the fire. Italian airplanes appeared and bombed the Ethiopian lines. A total of 107 Ethiopian soldiers died in the battle; the Italians lost 30 men, all Somalis.

Italy's hostile designs on Ethiopia were now undeniable. Haile Selassie appealed continuously to the League of Nations to resolve the matter before there was any further bloodshed. He was willing to accept a number of League proposals, all of which were favorable to Italy. But Mussolini rejected them all; he wanted a war. The League finally ordered its member states to halt arms sales to both countries, but the move hurt Ethiopia and helped Italy. Ethiopia was poorly armed and totally dependent on importing weapons from Europe; Italy had its own large weapons industry, which had already armed a 250,000-man invasion force that was poised and ready to invade from Eritrea and another force of 70,000 in Italian Somaliland.

The emperor's faith in the League of Nations was to no avail. In April 1935, Britain and France secretly agreed to allow Italy a free hand in Ethiopia in exchange for Mussolini's promise that he would not ally with Hitler should the German dictator start a war in Europe. Mussolini's promise would prove worthless; in 1940 he joined Hitler and declared war on Britain and France. Indeed, many years after World War II, Winston Churchill, the British prime minister during the war, looked back on Britain's failure to act against Mussolini's conquest of Ethiopia in 1935–36 and asked, "Could we have called Musso's bluff and at least postponed the war? The answer I'm sure is yes. We built Musso into a great power. . . . The fact that the nerve of the British

Government was not equal to the occasion played a part in leading to an infinitely more terrible war."

Yet despite all the indications that Mussolini was about to invade Ethiopia, Haile Selassie did not order mobilization of his troops until after the Italian forces crossed the Mareb River, the boundary between Eritrea and northern Ethiopia, on October 3, 1935. By then it was too late. The Italians, armed with the most advanced weaponry and supported by massive air power, routed the Ethiopian forces. Haile Selassie went to Dessie on November 28 to take personal command and was greeted by the sight of his demoralized forces scattered in the face of the Italian advance.

In the south, Italian tank forces from Somaliland rolled forward across the Ogaden and on to Harer. But incredibly, the southern tank offensive bogged down and came to a halt in late December, as much the result of the Italian military's inefficiency as the efforts of the Ethiopian infantry. Meanwhile up north, the invasion forces were slowed to a crawl by the forbidding mountains and ravines and were hemmed in by the armies of local rases and dejazmatches. The war had become a stalemate.

The road from Debre Markos to Dessie, an example of the rugged northern Ethiopian landscape that slowed the Italian advance at the end of 1935. Despite Italy's huge advantage in weaponry, the war was stalemated at the beginning of 1936.

In the first three months of 1936, the Italians used a new weapon to break the stalemate: poison gas. According to John H. Spencer, an American who at the time was Haile Selassie's personal adviser on international law:

> By March, following the series of Ethiopian victories, the campaign of aerial bombardment by liquid poison gas, mostly through spraying, was stepped up and soon reached apocalyptic proportions. The entire countryside was subjected to this rain of death. The fields through which the barefoot Ethiopian troops had to pass and the watercourses from which they drank were poisoned. Cattle, like humans, succumbed. The poison gas was a vesicant which raised hideous blisters on the feet and legs of the troops.

With the gas killing Ethiopian soldiers and civilians by the thousands, the Italians broke the stalemate and renewed the advance. The emperor decided to mount a counteroffensive from the town of Maytchew. But Haile Selassie, who personally led the counteroffensive, insisted on keeping the Ethiopian forces concentrated in a large mass. It was a mistake — guerrilla attacks would have been a more appropriate strategy against the armor and air power of the Italian forces — but the emperor's inexperience in military matters clouded his judgment. The poorly planned and miserably executed counteroffensive began on March 31 with a full-

Ethiopian troops, clad in modern uniforms but adhering to tradition by going barefoot. In 1936, Ethiopian forces totaled no more than 250,000 nationwide. Thousands were killed when Italian planes started spraying poison gas over Ethiopian troops. Civilian casualties were far higher.

scale Ethiopian attack, which started at 4:00 A.M.. The battle lasted until 11:00 P.M. that night, but it was futile. Italian planes bombarded the Ethiopian positions all day, finally silencing the imperial forces. After three more days of aerial attacks, the Ethiopians withdrew.

Now Haile Selassie and his forces were retreating in total disarray. They zigzagged through the mountains to avoid Italian planes as well as Welo peasants enraged by the news of the imprisoned Lij Iyasu's death. Rather than stay with his army to regroup and try to hold off the Italians, the emperor and his entourage went to the holy town of Lalibela to pray —and to figure out what to do next.

After two days they returned to Addis, a panicked city on the verge of outright chaos. There, on April 30, 1936, the council of ministers met to decide the future of the country. After a full day of deliberations they decided that the emperor, accompanied by his family and the necessary assistants, should leave the country immediately and proceed to the League of Nations in Geneva to appeal for help. The local lords would remain behind to direct the military resistance against the Italian occupiers.

At 4:00 A.M. on May 2, 1936, Haile Selassie, his family, and a retinue of high-ranking officials and important political prisoners boarded a train bound for Djibouti. At the city of Dire Dawa he told the prisoners they were pardoned, put them off the train, and asked them to fight for the resistance. When the train reached the desert, the emperor realized that the boat awaiting him could not accommodate the number of people he had with him, so he ordered some of his less important followers off the train. At the frontier with French-ruled Djibouti, the French border police forbade Haile Selassie's armed guards to enter the colony, so they too got off. The train finally arrived in Djibouti on the next day. The emperor and what was left of his retinue boarded a British ship and sailed away. Six years after his coronation, Emperor Haile Selassie had become the first Ethiopian monarch ever to choose to flee the country rather than stay behind and die with his men.

A body lies in the street in Addis Ababa following the Italian occupation of the city on May 6, 1936, four days after Haile Selassie fled it and Ethiopia. Haile Selassie became the first Ethiopian emperor ever, when faced with defeat, to flee the country rather than die alongside his soldiers.

6

The Throne Reclaimed

One week after Haile Selassie fled Ethiopia, Benito Mussolini stood on the balcony of his palace in Rome and told a huge crowd of cheering Italians:

> Today, May 9, of the fourteenth year of the Fascist era, the fate of Ethiopia is sealed. All the knots were cut by our shining sword, and the African victory stands in the history of our Fatherland whole and pure as the fallen legionnaires and those who survived dreamed and wanted it. At last Italy has her empire. A Fascist empire.

To the roar of the throng assembled below, the dictator proclaimed Italy's King Victor Emmanuel III the emperor of Ethiopia. Meanwhile, the true emperor of Ethiopia, Haile Selassie, was in Jerusalem, praying for the salvation of his country. Tens of thousands of Ethiopian soldiers and civilians had been killed in the 7 months of fighting, as against the loss of approximately 3,500 Italian troops, more than half of whom were Eritreans and Somalis.

After his moment in history Haile Selassie repaired to Bath, England, remaining there in exile.
—PETER SCHWAB
American historian

Haile Selassie leaving a reception hosted by a group of London women's organizations in September 1936. After addressing the League of Nations, the exiled emperor went to England, where he spent the next five years awaiting Britain's help in liberating Ethiopia.

Italy's King Victor Emmanuel III was proclaimed emperor of Ethiopia by Mussolini before a cheering crowd in Rome on May 9, 1936. Ironically, in 1924 Victor Emmanuel had welcomed Haile Selassie to Italy with the words: "I pray that God's blessings may descend upon Ethiopia."

Haile Selassie went on to Geneva to give his speech to the League of Nations, which within three years would collapse because of its ineffectiveness on Ethiopia and subsequent crises. After earning the sympathy and respect of most of the world but little else, the emperor, his family, and aides went to England to settle into exile at the resort and university town of Bath.

The British government gave the emperor and his party modest accommodations, but his efforts to convince the British to supply arms for the resistance back home were unsuccessful. The British authorities, still seeking to woo Mussolini to their side in case of war against Hitler, kept Haile Selassie under wraps. He would spend the next four years in Bath, quietly sustaining himself with the little money he brought from home and the contributions collected by friends of Ethiopia. At one point, he was so low on funds that he was forced to sell some of his personal effects. His aide John Spencer also reports that he secretly offered to negotiate recognition of the Italian conquest in exchange for several million dollars, but the Italians vetoed the idea.

The emperor was still an admired figure in most countries of the world, but back home his subjects, enduring a brutal occupation, forced labor, and mass executions, held little respect for him. Traditionally, the emperor in Ethiopia was the symbol of resistance; in the warfare to which Ethiopians were accustomed, an army disintegrates without a leader. Previous emperors had fought to the death, such as Tewodros, who killed himself rather than submit to the British, and Yohannes, who died in a battle against the Sudanese. Thus Haile Selassie's flight from the country in the middle of a war was considered a cowardly act by most Ethiopians.

Many nobles stayed behind to lead the resistance against the Italian occupation. Some, including Haile Selassie's longtime companion Ras Imru, had been captured and sent to prison camps (most of those who submitted to the conquerors suffered the same fate). Others, such as Ras Balcha, remained at large in the countryside, fighting a hit-and-run guerrilla war from mountain strongholds inaccessible to Italian tanks and planes. By the end of 1936, as Italian settlers arrived to colonize Ethiopia, the resistance was seriously disrupting the occupation. Many of the top figures in the resistance, among them several women, vowed to put another person on Haile Selassie's throne in case the Italians were ousted.

The situation changed for Haile Selassie in the second half of 1939. In September of that year Britain and France declared war on Germany — the formal beginning of World War II — and by May 1940 Winston Churchill, who was receptive to Haile Selassie's plight and who condemned Mussolini as "the jackal of Europe," became prime minister of Britain. On June 10, 1940, Mussolini declared war against an already defeated France and an isolated Britain. Haile Selassie suddenly became valuable to the desperate British as a symbol of antifascism.

Now Churchill moved quickly and decisively in support of the exiled emperor. On June 25, Haile Selassie was flown to Alexandria, Egypt, aboard a British plane and from there proceeded on to Khartoum, capital of the British-held Sudan. The British colonial authorities in Khartoum, who would have preferred to make Ethiopia a British possession

Haile Selassie at his home in exile in Bath, England. The British government provided the house but no money to the emperor and his family. Broke, Haile Selassie secretly offered to recognize the Italian conquest of Ethiopia in exchange for several million dollars. The deal never came off.

General Rodolfo Graziani, commander of Italian forces in Ethiopia and viceroy of the conquered nation, is given the fascist salute by Ethiopians in 1936. After a failed attempt was made on the viceroy's life, hundreds of leading Ethiopians were shot in what became known as the Graziani massacres.

after the Italians were ousted, did not want to let the emperor enter his kingdom. But after a six-month period in which the Italians were being soundly defeated in an attempt to overrun Egypt, Churchill sent word that Haile Selassie was to accompany the British-led forces preparing to invade Ethiopia from the Sudan.

The invasion began in January 1941. The main force consisted of British and South African troops, who attacked northern Eritrea; a smaller British-led group called the Gideon Force, manned by Ethiopian and Sudanese troops and accompanied by Haile Selassie, entered through Tigre province. The Gideon Force linked up with the resistance fighters led by Ras Kassa and raised the national flag on Ethiopian soil on January 20, 1941.

Victories came swiftly against the Italians, who were by now ragged and demoralized. On April 5, 1941, the southern units of the British force entered Addis Ababa, which the Italian army had abandoned the day before. On May 5, Haile Selassie returned to his capital amid a joyous welcome — five years to the day after it had fallen to the Italian forces. The emperor issued a proclamation urging Ethiopians not to carry out reprisals against any Italians who had been captured or left behind:

Do not reward evil for evil. Do not commit any act of cruelty like those which the enemy committed against us up to this present time. Do not allow the enemy any occasion to foul the good name of Ethiopia.

Haile Selassie hoped to pick up where he had left off as ruler of his country five years before, but the British authorities would have none of it. They considered Ethiopia a captured enemy territory whose fate would be decided in a peace conference after the war. In 1944, after three years of continuous appeals to Churchill, the British government finally restored Haile Selassie as emperor. The British, though, retained the right to police Ethiopia's borders and to determine much of the country's foreign policy.

The emperor therefore turned his attention to domestic policy, especially the resumption of his modernization program. His first measure, in 1942, put a tax on all lands; it was a move intended to replenish the national treasury and to strengthen the central government's hold on the provinces. The small farmers of the northern province of Gojam rebelled, and soon landlords and peasants in other northern provinces followed suit. The situation was so threatening that the emperor retreated from his position and issued a new proclamation exempting the northern provinces from tax payments.

But Haile Selassie did succeed in instituting a new system under which a governor-general would rule each province; the governor-general would not be free to rule however he pleased, as had been the practice under the traditional system, but would report all decisions to the emperor. The emperor further strengthened the central government by abolishing the armies of local and provincial lords. He ended the nobility's right to impose forced labor on the peasantry. The right of landlords to sit in judgment on local affairs was also abolished and replaced by a new judicial structure. To centralize land management, land surveys were instituted, and absentee landlords who failed to develop their holdings were threatened with confiscation.

Ras Kassa, who used his army to resist the Italian occupation in the north of Ethiopia. Long a personal ally of Haile Selassie, Ras Kassa was one of several leading resistance fighters operating from 1936 to 1941.

Winston Churchill, who became prime minister of Britain in May 1940, eight months after the outbreak of World War II. In June 1940, Italy declared war on Britain, prompting Churchill to send Haile Selassie to the Sudan to await a British-led invasion of Italian-occupied Ethiopia.

While he succeeded in establishing the governor-general system and abolishing the personal armies of the nobility, none of the other attacks against traditional local authority were fully carried out. They were too strongly opposed by the landlords, and Haile Selassie knew that he needed the landlords' support to survive politically. In the end, the objective of most of his reforms was centralization rather than liberalization.

The opposition to his measures led to a crisis in 1944, when one of the local lords, Dejazmatch Belay Zeleke, was arrested and charged with conspiring to overthrow Haile Selassie. Belay had been one of the resistance leaders who deeply resented the emperor's flight from Ethiopia in 1936. He and 60 others accused of participating in the plot were publicly hanged in the Addis Ababa market for all to see. The uncharacteristic ruthlessness of the emperor's act was effective: No other serious attempt would be made against his power for another 15 years.

Now that his position was secure on the domestic front, Haile Selassie renewed his landlocked empire's centuries-old effort to obtain territory on the Red Sea. In 1947 — two years after Mussolini's execution, Hitler's suicide, the defeat of Italy and Germany, and the conclusion of World War II — the emperor opened negotiations with Britain and other nations to acquire Eritrea and its 625-mile coastline.

Eritrea had been colonized by the Turks in the 1550s, the Egyptians in the 1870s, and the Italians in the 1890s before it was taken by the British in 1941. But Ethiopian emperors had always claimed Eritrea to be part of Ethiopia proper. The highland Eritreans share a common language, religion, and culture with the Tigreans of northern Ethiopia, and the two peoples were often ruled under the same monarchy, stretching as far back as the Axumite Kingdom of the 4th century A.D.

With the start of the 1950s, Haile Selassie used this historical claim at the United Nations (the newly organized successor to the defunct League of Nations) to request reunification of the two regions. Meanwhile, inside Eritrea, the emperor used the

Coptic Church and prominent Christian Eritreans to organize a party calling for a union between Ethiopia and Eritrea. Muslim Eritreans, who comprised about 40 percent of the population, generally opposed union, and some Eritrean Christians joined them in calling for an independent nation. The antiunionists argued that Eritreans had for centuries resisted efforts to incorporate the region into the Ethiopian Empire, and that the 50 years of Italian rule had transformed Eritrea into a more modern, outward-looking state than Ethiopia.

A commission was appointed by the United Nations to investigate the Eritrean situation. Based on its findings, the U.N. General Assembly adopted a plan under which Ethiopia and Eritrea would join as a federation on September 11, 1952 — almost what Haile Selassie sought. (The plan was designed by the United States; its support of the emperor's cause paid off in 1953, when Haile Selassie signed a treaty with the U.S. allowing it to establish a large naval base in Eritrea.) Under the U.N. arrangement, Eritrea was to have full control over its internal affairs, a stipulation consistently ignored by Haile Selassie once the plan went into effect. Finally, in 1962, the Christian-dominated Eritrean parliament voted to make Eritrea an Ethiopian province.

The emperor made gains in the southeast as well, successfully negotiating the return of the entire Ogaden region. Until 1948, the Ogaden had still been under the rule of the British, who considered uniting the region with the adjacent British Somaliland. Many among the Ogaden's large Somali population were angered by the decision, and starting in the 1960s they would lead a movement seeking to break away from Ethiopian rule.

Haile Selassie implemented a number of progressive social and economic reforms in the postwar years. A few hospitals were opened in the capital, and health-care clinics were established in major towns. Education was expanded both at the elementary and high school levels. In 1942 there were less than 2,000 pupils enrolled in educational institutions. By the end of the 1950's there were 643 public schools with close to 250,000 students. The

Haile Selassie outside Addis Ababa in April 1941, near the conclusion of the successful month-long campaign to retake Ethiopia. The liberation forces were led by British and South African troops, while Ras Kassa's resistance army linked up with smaller contingents of Ethiopian and Sudanese soldiers.

first institution of higher learning, the University College of Addis Ababa (later renamed Haile Selassie I University), was established in 1950 with just 21 students. Despite the modest size of the university, the emperor considered its opening to be the high point in his drive to modernize Ethiopia. It was housed in a palace donated by Haile Selassie, leaving the emperor to divide his time between his offices in Menilek's palace and his residence in the new Jubilee Palace.

Ethiopia's transportation system was greatly modernized. The nation inherited a number of roads built by the Italians to connect most provincial capitals with Addis Ababa and added to the total in the 1950s and 1960s. A more impressive achievement was made in air transport, which was highly advanced in comparison with the overall development of the country. By the early 1960s, the government airline offered flights between Ethiopia and 16 other countries. Domestic air service linked 39 points within Ethiopia, a vitally important breakthrough for a large nation with such a rugged geography.

Ethiopia's economy also showed reasonable growth during this period, mainly in urban areas involved in foreign trade. With Eritrea under Ethiopian rule, the nation's exports increased by 74 percent and its imports by 62 percent between 1952 and 1957. In 1945, Ethiopia's exports were worth $15 million; by 1957, exports reached $160 million; by 1968, $246 million. The growth of domestic manufacturing, though tiny compared to other countries even in Africa, showed improvement when measured by Ethiopian standards. In 1958 there were only 55 manufacturing concerns in Ethiopia, but in 1961 there were 95, employing approximately 29,000 Ethiopians and 900 foreigners.

In 1948 the emperor ended a 1,500-year-old tradition by convincing the Egyptian church to allow an Ethiopian to be named abuna. It was a nationalistic gesture that was popular with Ethiopia's Christians, but the Ethiopian Orthodox Church's right to impose taxes on the peasantry remained fundamentally unchanged.

The agricultural sector was the most neglected area in Haile Selassie's modernization scheme. As late as the 1960s, more than 90 percent of the population was still engaged in subsistence farming; that is, peasants were growing just enough crops to feed themselves and their families. In addition, the peasants handed over more than half of their produce to landlords and the church.

Agriculture provided the basis for Ethiopia's entire social structure. Class distinctions — from weavers and blacksmiths on the bottom of the social scale, up through the ranks of artisans, peasant farmers, traders, merchants, local lords, and provincial lords, to the emperor himself — were all based in some way on ownership of land or its produce. Although it was possible for someone to move up the scale through military, educational, or business achievement, the land-ownership system itself remained basically unchanged. The landholding system perpetuated the dominance of the landlord class and the church over the peasants, the majority of whom remained impoverished and powerless. The system was so much a part of Ethiopian society that few realized it was, in effect, an instrument of oppression.

The emperor's reforms were vigorous by Ethiopian standards in many areas, but he never made any substantial attempts to reform agriculture. It was the most basic and important feature of economic life for peasant and noble alike, and the one

As British military officials look on, Ethiopian troops prostrate themselves before Haile Selassie in Addis soon after the ouster of the Italians in 1941. Britain did not restore full sovereignty to Ethiopia until 1948.

An Ethiopian college student teaching young students how to read. Haile Selassie established the country's first university and sent many promising students abroad to study, but he did little to educate the general population. The illiteracy rate in Ethiopia was estimated at 85 percent.

most bound by traditional laws and customs. The restructuring of Ethiopian agricultural practice was too radical a step for Haile Selassie ever to take — if indeed he could even have conceived of it.

The emperor was quite aware that his other modernization plans required an element of political liberalization. In 1954 he appointed a commission to draft a new constitution that would give the appearance of opening the political system to the public without in any way limiting his total control over the nation.

The constitution was ready in 1955, in time for the 25th anniversary of Haile Selassie's coronation. Designed after European and American models, it provided for freedom of religion, speech, assembly, and the press — but only within the limits of the law, which were not clearly defined. All power, of course, ultimately resided in the person of the emperor, "the elect of God," although citizens were given the right, in accordance with tradition, to petition the emperor in person.

The constitution did not allow for political parties as most foreign observers had hoped, but that was not considered a weakness among Ethiopians, even among the most enlightened elements in society. In fact, as the emperor's longtime American aide, John Spencer, observed, "political parties were feared to take regional coloring and hence [to be] undesirable to the unity of Ethiopia." The one-party system would become the common political structure throughout most of Africa after nations on that continent gained their independence in the 1960s and 1970s.

The new Ethiopian constitution also broadened the powers of the two-chamber parliament. The upper house was to be appointed by the emperor himself. The lower house was to be elected by popular vote — but only property-owners would be allowed to run for office, effectively guaranteeing the emperor control of both houses. When the first elections in Ethiopia's history were held in 1957, virtually all of those elected were from the landlord class. They were eager to protect their own interests from the threat of modernization rather than to advance a progressive agenda.

As the 1950s drew to a close, Haile Selassie had still not designated a successor. Although nearly 70 years old, he was still a vigorous man who exerted compulsive control over every aspect of his nation's life. Most Ethiopians thought that a successor should be designated to avoid chaos if the emperor died suddenly, but he was known to have doubts about his oldest son and the likeliest candidate to succeed to the throne, Crown Prince Asfa Wossen, who was seen by most as a weak, vacillating man.

Haile Selassie's second son, Ras Makonnen, was his favorite; he had appointed him to govern Harer. Many believed that Makonnen would be chosen as the next emperor, but he died in an auto crash in 1957. As for the other children of Haile Selassie and Empress Menen, Princess Zanabe Worq had died in 1933 and Princess Tsahay in 1942; Princess Tenegne Worq, their eldest child, and Prince Sahle Selassie, their youngest, were still alive.

But Haile Selassie seemed to have no interest in designating any of his three surviving children as his succesor. With the dawn of the 1960s, the emperor showed no sign of loosening his grip on power.

Ballot boxes for Ethiopia's first election, held in September 1957. Despite the elections, Haile Selassie retained full control over all political and monetary affairs. As was the case with all previous emperors, he, his family, and the nobility skimmed money from most state projects and private businesses throughout his reign.

7

Africa's Elder Statesman

The complete control Haile Selassie exercised over the political life of Ethiopia was a remarkable phenomenon. If a top official threatened to become too powerful he might demote him to some provincial outpost of little importance, or he might elevate a low-ranking rival of the official to a high position. No one at Haile Selassie's court knew who would be promoted or demoted, and officials expended all their energies trying to gain the emperor's trust or trying to erode his trust in other officials. Thus Haile Selassie played his advisers against one another unerringly, a skill he had begun to develop as a boy at Menilek's court. His mastery of intrigue was the secret to his remarkably long reign.

The emperor never associated himself with failed policies, even when he initiated them. The successful programs, on the other hand, were always attributed to his genius. He was known to be a hardworking and energetic man with a remarkable memory for even the smallest detail, never writing or signing orders or documents. Some believe that this

Ethiopia has need of no one; she stretches out her hands to God.
—EMPEROR MENELIK II

Haile Selassie converses with Egyptian president Gamal Abdel Nasser and other African heads of state during a 1964 Organization of African Unity (OAU) conference in Cairo. During the 1960s the emperor became a leading figure in international diplomacy, particularly as a spokesman for emerging African nations.

Haile Selassie with the governor of Brazil's São Paulo state in December 1960. Soon after this photo was taken, the emperor learned that back in Addis Ababa the Imperial Guard had announced his overthrow and the establishment of a new government dedicated to reform and the eradication of Ethiopia's crushing poverty.

was a deliberate ploy to dissociate himself from his own decisions in case denial was necessary. If so, it worked: The common people of Ethiopia loved Haile Selassie and were awed by him, both because they respected him and because throughout the nation's history the emperor had always been a revered figure.

What Haile Selassie did not see, however, was that his push for modernization would stir an appetite in his people for more significant reforms. In the late 1950s the reform-minded people in the capital saw that the emperor was not serious about implementing the new constitution. The dissatisfaction grew slowly and finally led to a coup attempt in December 1960, when Haile Selassie and a large contingent from his court were on a state visit to Brazil.

The coup attempt was led by the Neway brothers, Mengistu and Germame. Mengistu Neway was the commander of the Imperial Guards, the elite military unit whose assignment was the personal protection of the emperor. Germame Neway had gone to university in the United States on a scholarship paid for by the Ethiopian government and had returned to become a member of the young, educated elite Haile Selassie appointed to key government positions. He was sent to govern a region in Sidamo province, an area where coffee beans, an important export crop, were grown. There, without the approval of the emperor, he ordered the building of schools and gave unused land to peasants. Haile

Selassie recalled him and punished him for these offenses by reassigning him to govern an arid region in Harer.

With the emperor thousands of miles away, the Neway brothers struck. They rounded up all the conservative nobles they could find and held them prisoner, shooting several of those whom they considered most dangerous. They then gave Asfa Wossen a statement to read over the radio:

> In the last years, stagnancy has reigned in Ethiopia. An atmosphere of discontent and disappointment has spread among peasants, merchants, office workers, in the army and police, among students, all through society. There is no progress in any quarter. This results from the fact that a handful of dignitaries have locked themselves into a course of egoism and nepotism, instead of working for the good of the whole community. The people of Ethiopia have waited for the day when poverty and backwardness would cease to be, but nothing has been achieved after innumerable promises. No other nation has borne so much in patience. . . .
>
> The few selfish persons who fight merely for their own interests and for personal power, who are obstacles to progress, and who, like a cancer, impede the nation's development are now replaced.

The crown prince announced that his father had been deposed and that he, Asfa Wossen, was now emperor of Ethiopia; Ras Imru, his father's old friend, was named prime minister. When Haile Selassie heard the news in Brazil, he boarded a plane and headed for Liberia to await further developments.

The Neways were backed by the 6,000-man Imperial Guard (but not by the army or the air force, which had several times more troops available) and by the students at the university in Addis. The rebels' demands for a constitutional monarchy with genuine democracy, fundamental economic and agricultural reform, and a meaningful effort to end the chronic poverty of the vast majority of the nation's population found a welcome reception at the university.

The body of an executed rebel leader hangs in the Addis marketplace in December 1960. The coup attempt was crushed after three days of fighting in which several leading figures in Haile Selassie's government and 500 rebels were killed. Crown prince Asfa Wossen, a participant in the failed coup, was pardoned.

The army and air force units arrived in Addis three days after the coup attempt began, and fighting broke out. It quickly turned into a rout. Nearly 500 Guardsmen were killed and more than 3,000 arrested. The Neways and a handful of others escaped to the mountains outside Addis but were captured a week later by peasants. Germame committed suicide rather than surrender.

By that time Haile Selassie had returned to the capital. Government officials, military officers, and students came to the throne room to personally pledge their loyalty to him. He pardoned Ras Imru and restored him to his former post. He also pardoned Asfa Wossen, who claimed he had been forced to give the radio speech at gunpoint, but thereafter Haile Selassie always regarded him with suspicion. The emperor was not so lenient with Mengistu Neway and the other captured leaders of the rebellion: They were hanged in the Addis market, the third and last time the emperor would order the public execution of his opponents.

Despite the failure of the coup, it marked a very important transition in Ethiopian political history.

It awakened a host of groups demanding far more fundamental reforms than Haile Selassie was willing to implement. From 1960 on, the emperor could no longer be seen as a progressive modernizer; he would have to ally with the conservatives to preserve the monarchy.

Haile Selassie rebounded from the 1960 coup attempt — and from the death of Empress Menen in 1961 and Prince Sahle Selassie in 1962 — by devoting his attention to African affairs. He hoped to paper over Ethiopia's domestic troubles by scoring a number of diplomatic successes that would enhance his international stature. The emperor's efforts to be recognized as a world statesman had begun as early as the 1920s, but until 1960, his platform had never been in the area of African politics.

Traditionally, neither Ethiopian emperors nor the Ethiopian people had ever closely identified themselves with other Africans, and indeed tended to view them with contempt. Many Christian Ethiopians looked down upon black Africans as dark-

The Jubilee Palace. Although Haile Selassie made enormous strides in bringing Ethiopia into the 20th century, he was still very much an autocratic monarch who ruled according to the ancient traditions of the Ethiopian monarchy. Many of the young Ethiopians whose education he had sponsored began to see him and the monarchy as hopelessly outdated.

Haile Selassie with U.S. president John F. Kennedy (right), U.S. vice-president Lyndon Johnson (rear), Kennedy's mother, Rose, and Johnson's wife, Lady Bird Johnson, in Washington, D.C., in October 1963. In the postwar years the emperor negotiated with the world's most powerful leaders, including U.S. presidents Eisenhower and Nixon and Soviet first secretary Brezhnev.

skinned pagans (even within the nation, Ethiopians with dark complexions faced considerable prejudice). It was an attitude stemming largely from Ethiopia's historic isolation behind its mountain walls, from its unique position as Africa's only Christian land, and from the fact that when the country was opened to foreigners — beginning in the 16th century and continuing on into Haile Selassie's reign — no independent African nations existed. Thus, most of Ethiopia's dealings, even in areas such as delineating her borders with neighboring African colonies, were negotiated with European powers.

Yet African nationalists looked to Ethiopia and Haile Selassie as symbols of African independence and black liberation. When the decolonization process started in Africa in the late 1950s, Haile Selassie saw an opportunity to play an important role in regional politics. In 1958, the year after Ghana became the first African colony to be granted independence, the emperor proposed the establishment of an African development bank. It marked the earliest attempt to set up a continental organization to assist African states in their efforts toward self-rule.

In the early 1960s, as the number of free African nations grew in number, ideological differences divided them into two camps. The Casablanca group — led by such prominent pan-Africanists as Ghana's Kwame Nkrumah and Egypt's Gamal-Abdel Nasser — advocated a revolutionary program requiring independent African countries to openly support and arm anticolonial movements until all of Africa was free from European domination. Generally hostile to Great Britain, which until recently had administered most of their countries as colonies, and to the United States, which they believed was guilty of exploiting small nations for the profit of American commercial interests, the Casablanca group embraced socialism and tended to seek the support of the Soviet Union and the People's Republic of China.

This was too radical for the taste of Haile Selassie and other conservative African leaders, who became known as the Monrovia group. They organized their own conference in 1961 in Monrovia, the capital of Liberia. The Monrovia conference was sponsored by

Nigeria, Cameroon, Liberia, and Togo and included most of the former French African colonies. Although they too supported the anticolonial movements, the nations of the Monrovia group had close economic ties with France and did not want to jeopardize them. They also sought to strengthen ties with the United States, the world's wealthiest nation.

Haile Selassie, though more sympathetic to the Monrovia group than to the Casablanca group, stayed aloof from the dispute between the two ideological camps. Instead, he professed neutrality and argued for African unity on a broad platform stressing the common problems and concerns that all Africans shared. In the United Nations, Ethiopian delegates strongly condemned South Africa, where a white minority government denied basic human rights to the black majority. The emperor also advocated the limitation of French nuclear tests in the Sahara Desert and supported the cause of Algerian nationalists fighting against France for independence.

Haile Selassie founded the OAU in 1963 with Addis Ababa as its headquarters. With the emperor in this 1967 photo are (left to right) Presidents Kayibanda of Rwanda, Obote of Uganda, Bokassa of the Central African Republic, Nyerere of Tanzania, Haile Selassie, Kaunda of Zambia, and Kenyatta of Kenya, Prime Minister Egal of Somalia, and President El-Azhari of the Sudan.

In late 1962, the emperor invited all the leaders of independent African nations to Addis for a conference on African unity — the first time such a conference had ever been held. It convened in May 1963 and was a complete success. The emperor presented his guests with a carefully worked out and uncontroversial agenda, his lack of commitment to the ideological issues that split the continent giving him credibility as a mediator. The conference resulted in the formation of the Organization of African Unity (OAU), and Addis Ababa was chosen as its permanent headquarters.

Haile Selassie became Africa's undisputed elder statesman and acknowledged spokesman, not only in the United Nations but also in all forms of diplomatic exchange with the United States and other countries around the world. He managed to win the respect of even the most radical pan-Africanist leaders like Nkrumah, who had been very critical of the emperor's policies at home and his close ties with the West.

The newly acquired international prestige left Haile Selassie more comfortable with his new image in African politics than he was at home. He devoted most of his time to traveling around the continent and the world rather than concentrating on the pressing problems of ignorance and poverty in his own country. He successfully mediated the Moroccan-Algerian border dispute of 1963 and defused the potentially explosive situation between Ghana and Guinea after the fall of Nkrumah in 1966. In the spirit of the OAU charter, which affirmed the borders of all existing African nations, he intervened on the side of the Nigerian government during the bloody civil war against its separatist province of Biafra.

At the same time, Ethiopia had border problems of its own. After Haile Selassie accepted Eritrea as Ethiopia's 14th province in 1962, Eritrean rebel groups sprang up. Fighting broke out between the rebels and government troops. It was the beginning of a bitter and costly war that would continue beyond the 1980s — the longest continuously fought war in the world. Meanwhile in the southeast, Somalia (the independent nation formed in 1960 from the old colonies of British Somaliland and Italian Somaliland) began to press Ethiopia to give up the Ogaden region for incorporation into Somalia. Tensions between the two nations would simmer until 1977, when open warfare broke out.

Haile Selassie needed to upgrade his military forces in order to hold Eritrea and the Ogaden. The task was eagerly taken up by the United States government, which regarded its naval base in the Eritrean port city of Mitsiwa as vitally important for controlling the Red Sea. Hundreds of American advisers were sent to train the Ethiopian armed forces. As the American historian Peter Schwab points out, the United States provided $200 million in military

Eritrean rebels during the 1980s. The former Italian colony was made Ethiopia's 14th province in 1962, realizing the emperor's long-held goal of gaining territory on the Red Sea. Most Eritrean Muslims and many Christians protested; a bloody guerrilla war broke out and continued through the 1980s — the longest-running war of the century.

The emperor examines a lamb at a U.S. agricultural research station in Maryland in 1969. He showed little interest, however, in reforming the traditional landowning arrangements in Ethiopia, where peasants continued to turn over large portions of their harvests to the central government, the landlords and the clergy of the Ethiopian Orthodox Church.

aid to Ethiopia between 1963 and 1974, half of the entire total spent by the U.S. for military aid in all of Africa. Substantial military assistance to Ethiopia was also provided by the Israelis, who feared that an independent, Muslim Eritrea would cut off Israel's access to the sea. By the end of the 1960s, the empire's armed forces numbered 45,000 and its police forces 30,000 — one of the largest militaries in Africa.

The military buildup was primarily intended to keep Ethiopia's various ethnic groups from rebelling. The emperor also tried to use the ideology of African unity to dampen regionalist sentiments.

The government-controlled radio exhorted Ethiopians to think of themselves as Africans and Ethiopians rather than Tigreans, Shewans, Somalis, Muslim Oromos, Christian Oromos, or Eritreans. But the continuing poverty of most Ethiopians kept the possibility of rebellion alive.

As more and more foreigners visited Ethiopia and stayed in the country to work at the OAU and the other international organizations located in the capital, they discovered a shocking contradiction between the image and reality of the emperor's domestic policies. Most Africans, before they had a chance to visit Ethiopia, took it for granted that the diplomatic center of the continent would be much more economically and socially developed than the newly independent African countries. Since they tended to regard their own countries' backwardness as the result of colonialism, they naturally expected that Ethiopia, which had escaped colonialism, would be more advanced and less ridden by poverty. But once in Ethiopia they found that the empire was at a level of social and economic development much lower than that of many African countries.

Pressure mounted against the emperor to come to grips with the 85 percent rate of illiteracy, the absence of elementary medical care, and, most important of all, the poverty in which more than 90 percent of the population lived. What was needed was a fundamental restructuring of the economy, particularly a program of land reform in which the enormous holdings of the nobility would be broken up and redistributed to the peasants. Such reforms were suggested by foreign supporters of Haile Selassie and by reform-minded Ethiopians. But the emperor was not receptive to any such ideas.

By 1967, Haile Selassie was 75 years old and in no mood to step down from power to allow a smooth transition to a younger generation. He was getting more intransigent to the advice given by even his closest aides. The cries for reform that were heard from all sectors of society were totally ignored by an emperor whose lifelong belief in pomp and personal prestige now completely overshadowed his interest in issues and leadership.

In 1967 and 1968 the absolute power of Haile Selassie was shown to be an illusion and its chimerical status became obvious to all the major contending forces in Ethiopia.
—PETER SCHWAB
American historian

8

"Am I Supposed to Go Like This?"

By the end of the 1960s, student groups in Ethiopia had openly begun to advocate the overthrow of Haile Selassie's regime. The American historian Randi R. Balsvik notes that as late as 1968

> the average university student still regarded the Emperor with respect and even admiration, despite general opposition to the government. This distinction between the Emperor's persona and his government started changing in 1969, when students started accusing Haile Selassie of lying about the state of affairs in the country. In student publications, he was accused of "flight" in the Ethiopian-Italian war of 1935–41. In politics, he was held to be a master of divide-and-rule tactics. His pompousness and claim to divinity were also ridiculed.

But if Haile Selassie was no longer universally exalted at home, abroad his reputation was growing — and among one group his claim to divinity was taken very seriously indeed. It had begun with Italy's

---

Two servants tend to their duties while Haile Selassie receives an ambassador at the imperial court in the 1970s. Life at court had changed little after more than 50 years of the emperor's reign, with officials vying for Haile Selassie's favor during the daily routine of audiences and ceremonies.

A faithful subject hurls himself to the ground upon the approach of the emperor's Mercedes-Benz in 1974. Until the final months of Haile Selassie's reign, most Ethiopians continued to believe that he was the "Elect of God" and viewed him with appropriate reverence.

1935 invasion of Ethiopia, which triggered tremendous passion among blacks in the Western Hemisphere. The fall of Ethiopia to white colonialists meant that, aside from Liberia, the colonization of black Africa was complete. The symbolic importance of a free Ethiopia was so great that thousands of blacks in New York City volunteered to go to Ethiopia to fight against Italy.

In Jamaica, the movement to liberate blacks from the political and cultural oppression of Europeans led to a search for an alternative religion outside the European form of Christianity, which was considered to be one of the many instruments of white domination. Already by 1930, when European and U.S. newspapers reported the coronation of Haile Selassie in front of European dignitaries, many blacks in Jamaica had "replaced the white God in heaven . . . with the Coptic version of a God who was both divine and human," as the Jamaican historian Horace Campbell put it. Among many black Jamaicans, who called themselves "Rastafari," Haile Selassie came to be regarded as a divine figure, a messiah sent by God, who would one day lead a revolt of blacks against whites.

Haile Selassie's plane touched down in Jamaica for a state visit in 1966, and a tumultuous crowd of more than 100,000 turned out at the airport. When the door opened and the emperor stepped onto the top of the ramp, he saw many in the crowd fall to their knees. Deeply moved by their devotion, he watched, then went back inside the plane until the authorities managed to open a path at the bottom of the stairway.

Back in Ethiopia, though, few people were aware that halfway around the world their emperor was regarded as a divine figure. Student protests became a regular feature in the capital, and Haile Selassie's government reacted in a repressive manner. On the evening of December 28, 1969, one of the leaders of the student movement was murdered by unknown assailants. Students blamed the government for the murder and organized a protest rally the next day. Imperial bodyguards opened fire on the demonstrators, killing 23 and wounding 157.

The mounting frustration of the educated elite was fueled by economic stagnation and growing poverty in the urban centers of the country. The stagnant national economy could no longer provide adequate jobs for the few graduates of the nation's only university. The unemployment rate among high school graduates reached crisis proportions, leaving a large number of angry unemployed youths in the major cities and towns of the country. Amid all this, Haile Selassie celebrated his 80th birthday in an extravagant display, wasting what many thought to be the country's limited resources.

In the meantime, the rural population was suffering from drought, crop failure, and the threat of widespread famine. The land of northern Ethiopia, traditionally held by the peasants in small communal and family farms, was no longer able to sustain the population. With tax rates remaining roughly the same, peasants often had little of their harvests left for themselves after giving over the required amounts to the local lords, church, or central government.

In March 1973, a combination of bad weather and the local lords' hoarding of crop surpluses led to

A Rastafarian at his Jamaican home in the 1980s. The religion (its name is derived from *Ras Tafari*) holds that Haile Selassie is the African king and divine messianic figure who will someday lead oppressed blacks in the struggle to overcome white domination.

Addis Ababa policemen rough up a protestor during a student demonstration in the 1970s. Beginning in 1969, when police killed 23 protesting students, Haile Selassie I University (the nation's only institution of higher learning) became the center of antigovernment sentiment.

starvation in the north. It became common knowledge in the capital that thousands of farmers from the famine-struck provinces of Welo and Tigre had marched toward the capital, only to be driven back by the military and put in makeshift refugee camps. Haile Selassie's government, worried about its image, denied the existence of the famine and did nothing to alleviate it.

Tens of thousands of Ethiopians died of starvation. It was only after Ethiopian students sneaked foreign journalists into the northern provinces that the famine became public knowledge. Foreign aid started pouring in immediately, but it only had the effect of stepping up official Ethiopian denials of the famine. Even the most ardent foreign supporters of Haile Selassie's regime were appalled and embarrassed. The United States government and its allies, the emperor's major foreign supporters, started to distance themselves from his regime. Haile Selassie's ministers continued to deny that the famine existed, attributing the mass movement of starving people to the cities as "the peasant's natural propensity to migrate."

Still reeling from international outrage over the famine, the government received another shock late in 1973, when the price of oil quadrupled in international markets. Ethiopia's treasury was depleted by the skyrocketing cost of purchasing oil, and the government responded by imposing serious austerity measures. The price of most commodities shot up, especially gasoline prices, which doubled. Cabdrivers in Addis Ababa called a strike to demand a reduction in the price of gasoline.

Massive demonstrations in the capital and other major cities followed as workers demanded pay increases to recover the buying power they had lost to inflation. The national teachers' union struck, demanding the repeal of an education reform bill that they considered to be unfair to children of the poor. Finally the army troops mutinied, arresting their officers, calling for pay hikes, and demanding

A poster distributed in Addis Ababa by students in 1973 during the famine that led to the death of perhaps 200,000 northern peasants; it contrasts images of a starving peasant and the emperor's dogs being fed meat from a platter.

የሚወዳትና (?) የሚወዳቸው ሕዝባቸው የሚቀምሱ ፍሬፍ እጦ በረሃብ አለንጋ እየተጠበስ ለሠራኸትና ለፍትግ እንደ ጋ እርደታ ሊደረግለት ይቆርና መረበም ግለቁም እንደታወጡ ተደርጎ ከአንድ መጽሐፍ በሕዝብ በላይ እነዚሁ ሆ ልት ወ ሽቸቸ እ ንደማ ታየው እ የተፈፀመ ይዳስ በ እ ረ ስ ጸ ን ም

Haile Selassie with famine victims in 1973. For months, the government denied that there was a famine. It admitted that there was a problem only after outraged students snuck a British television crew into the drought-ravaged north. Food shortages had been worsened by landlords, who hoarded tons of grain.

the right to burial (soldiers killed in fighting against the Eritrean guerrillas were left where they had fallen; only the bodies of officers were picked up for burial).

Haile Selassie wanted to appease the opposition by removing ministers at the top level of government, but he was reluctant to take that unseemly step. The prime minister came to his rescue by graciously offering his resignation and that of his cabinet, which the emperor quickly accepted. Although the move was merely cosmetic, as Haile Selassie was still making all the major decisions in his old autocratic way, most Ethiopians continued to believe that the ministers were the ones responsible for the calamities. The emperor, they continued to believe, was a just man who had been misled.

By this time, however, the low-level officers and soldiers all around the country had chosen representatives and sent them to Addis to coordinate the demands of the armed forces. A *derg*, or committee, of more than 120 military men was formed to study the situation in the capital and report back to the troops as soon as possible. Neither the derg nor the troops who elected its members knew at the time that they would bring about the death of an old monarchy that had lost the political instinct to survive.

The emperor appointed a new prime minister, his longtime aide Endalkachew Makonnen, who immediately raised the salaries of the military and reduced the price of gasoline. But it was too late: The derg had already arrested most of the officials of the previous government on charges of corruption. The new government pleaded with the derg to release the prisoners, but the army officers totally ignored the pleas.

A virtual dual power system ensued for several months. One center was the nominal government of Prime Minister Endalkachew, who tried to control the situation by promising extensive reforms. The other center was the derg, which was now more assertive and increasingly willing to bring about a total break with the old regime. There was no indication that the aging emperor was in any way involved in resolving this potentially disastrous problem. He seemed to be content with the verbal assurances he received from the government and the derg, both of which declared their loyalty to him, and did nothing.

In February 1974, John H. Spencer, the American who had served as Haile Selassie's adviser on international law on and off since 1936, came to Addis for a visit with the emperor. Spencer noted that the emperor's legendary memory was failing, his regal bearing was gone, his "charisma extinguished":

> It became apparent to me during the course of our conversation that Haile Selassie was already retreating into a dream world. To me, who had known him for nearly 40 years, he appeared to have become disturbingly inarticulate. I withdrew with the piercing realization that the curtain of senility had dropped.

In April 1974, the emperor finally named his successor: his grandson Prince Zara Jacob, the son of Asfa Wossen, who was ailing and living in Switzerland. But the decision came too late to make any difference. In June, the military learned that the Endalkachew government was preparing to get rid of the derg. The officers responded with a new wave

Demonstrators applaud as Prime Minister Endalkachew Makonnen is burned in effigy in March 1974. Haile Selassie did nothing when in June a military committee started rounding up leading government officials and nobles for jail or execution. Many believe that by this point the emperor was senile.

of arrests, and more than 100 leading figures in the government and the nobility were rounded up and held in the basement of the Menelik Palace. The derg took over the radio and television stations. It proclaimed a new movement for renewal, under the motto *Ethiopia tikdem* ("Ethiopia first"), and informed listeners which ministers had been arrested and why. The derg continued to justify all its actions in the name of the emperor. Haile Selassie, apparently not understanding what was going on, went through his daily rounds in the now nearly deserted Jubilee Palace dressed in full military uniform.

On September 11 there were more arrests, including that of Princess Tenegne Worq. That night, Ethiopian television showed a British Broadcasting Corporation film of the Ethiopian famine — the same film that first broke the story to the world — made by a British television journalist, Jonathan Dimbleby. After the report was finished, commentators read a statement from the derg accusing the emperor of embezzling millions of dollars from the government treasury and of refusing to give back the money he owed the country.

Major Mengistu Haile Mariam and General Tafari Benti, leaders of the *derg* (military committee) that overthrew Haile Selassie in September 1974. By 1977, Mengistu had eliminated Benti and the rest of his opponents; he ruled a famine- and war-torn Ethiopia through the 1980s.

The next morning, several military trucks pulled up in front of the palace. Army officers in full combat gear, accompanied by an unwilling Ras Imru, entered the chamber where Haile Selassie had been since dawn. One of them approached the emperor and read a statement. It was brief and to the point:

> Even though the people treated the throne in good faith as a symbol of unity, Haile Selassie I took advantage of its authority, dignity, and honor for his own personal ends. As a result, the country found itself in a state of poverty and disintegration. Moreover, an eighty-two-year-old Monarch, because of his age, is incapable of meeting his responsibilities. Therefore, His Imperial Majesty Haile Selassie I is being disposed of as of September 12, 1974, and power assumed by the Provisional Military Committee. Ethiopia above all!

Thus ended over half a century of rule by Emperor Haile Selassie. The officers led the King of the Kings of Ethiopia to a green Volkswagen parked in front of the palace. "You can't be serious," the emperor is reported to have said. "Am I supposed to go like this?" He then got into the car and took a place on the back seat. The VW drove away, taking Haile Selassie to spend whatever was left of his life imprisoned in the rooms of the old Menilek palace.

Haile Selassie was never again seen in public. Those who knew him remembered him as a man of contradictions. He was known to have been intelligent, hardworking, gentle, thoughtful, and remarkably loyal to those he considered his friends and allies. But he was also known to have been egotistical, addicted to pomp and self-glorification, and far more concerned about the well-being of the animals he kept than the peasants he ruled. As a former prime minister noted, the emperor was "beyond doubt, even beyond imagination, the most selfish and grasping man I have ever known."

When Haile Selassie took power in 1916, Ethiopia was a patchwork of regions ruled, as it had been for centuries, by a tangled network of feudal lords. By the time he was removed in 1974, he had transformed Ethiopia into a modern nation. He had be-

By August 1974 the Derg had become convinced that Haile Selassie had to be disposed.
—JOHN H. SPENCER
international law advisor to
Haile Selassie

gun by implementing reforms and abolishing many of the cruel practices of the past, by opening the country to the outside world, and by bringing Ethiopia under the control of a central government. He ended by upholding the archaic traditional values of which he was a product, refusing to surrender power to the younger generation whose education he had promoted. In the end he was a victim of change, the very force that he himself had long ago unleashed in Ethiopia.

In the violent years that followed the overthrow of Haile Selassie, Ethiopia very nearly disintegrated. Two months after the emperor was escorted from his palace, the chairman of the derg was killed in a gun battle. A new group of officers took over the leadership; shortly thereafter, 60 of the imprisoned members of the old government and high nobility, including Endalkachew Makonnen, were machine-gunned. The derg declared Ethiopia a socialist state and undertook many reforms, distributing land to the peasants and nationalizing all foreign-owned businesses. Still, there was widespread violent opposition to the regime. A 1977 palace coup left Major Mengistu Haile Mariam the leader of the derg, which then carried out a series of purges that ended in the chaotic "Red Terror," in which thousands died in pro- and antigovernment fighting.

Later in 1977, Soviet-backed Somalia invaded Ethiopia through the Ogaden and got as far as the gates of Harer. Mengistu appealed to the Soviets for aid. They agreed to abandon Somalia and back Ethiopia, and Cuban troops arrived to repel the invasion. Mengistu expelled the Americans, who switched their support to Somalia. The Mengistu government started to lose the civil war in Eritrea. Other separatist movements sprang up to redress historic resentment of Shewan domination or to oppose the regime, and as many as seven guerrilla wars broke out throughout the nation. Ethiopia was recognized as the world's poorest nation, yet 40 percent of its budget went to the military, which had become one of Africa's largest. In 1983, drought and the ravages of warfare caused massive crop failures.

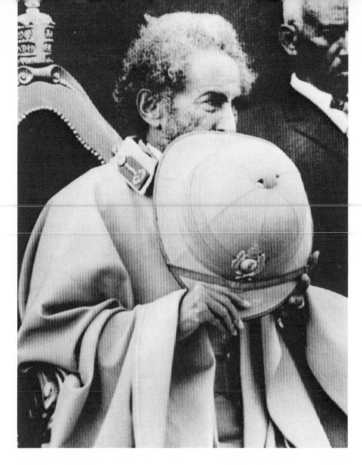

Emperor Haile Selassie was deposed on September 12, 1974, and driven away from the Jubilee Palace in the back of a Volkswagen as the citizens of the capital shouted "thief!" He was held in a room in Menilek's palace and never seen in public again. He died on August 28, 1975, and was buried in an unmarked grave on the palace grounds.

Approximately 12 million of Ethiopia's 42 million people suffered from the resulting famine. Over the next four years, hundreds of thousands of Ethiopians — perhaps millions — died of starvation. Millions more fled to refugee camps in the Sudan and Somalia.

On August 28, 1975, Ethiopian radio announced the death from circulatory failure of the former emperor of Ethiopia, Haile Selassie I. That same day, as the noise of automobile traffic and airplanes filled the air, a grave was dug on the grounds of Menilek's palace, which young Tafari Makonnen had first seen from the back of a mule after a 16-day journey over roadless deserts and mountains.

His body was lowered without ceremony into the grave, which was filled with earth and left unmarked. People in the capital heard the news and went on with their business. It seemed as though they had already forgotten about him.

Further Reading

Balsvik, Randi R. *Haile Selassie's Students. The Intellectual and Social Background to Revolution, 1952–1977.* East Lansing: Michigan State University Press, 1985.

Campbell, Horace. *Rasta and Resistance.* Trenton, NJ: Africa World Press, 1987.

Clapham, Christopher. *Haile Selassie's Government.* London: Longmans, Green, 1969.

Hartenian, Larry. *Benito Mussolini.* New York: Chelsea House, 1985.

Jacobs, Virginia Lee. *Roots of Rastafari.* San Diego: Avant Books, 1985.

Kapuściński, Ryszard. *The Emperor: The Downfall of an Autocrat.* New York: Random House, 1983.

Last, G., and Pankhurst, R. *A History of Ethiopia in Pictures.* London: Oxford University Press, 1965.

Marcus, Harold G. *Haile Selassie I.* Berkeley: University of California Press, 1987.

Mockler, Anthony. *Haile Selassie's War.* New York: Random House, 1984.

Pankhurst, Richard. *Let's Visit Ethiopia.* London: Burke, 1984.

Prouty, Chris. *Empress Taytu and Emperor Menelik II: Ethiopia 1883–1910.* Trenton, NJ: Red Sea Press, 1986.

Schwab, Peter. *Haile Selassie I: Ethiopia's Lion of Judah.* Chicago: Nelson-Hall, 1979.

Selassie, Bereket Habte. *Conflict and Intervention in the Horn of Africa.* New York: Monthly Review Press, 1980.

Selassie, Haile. *My Life and Ethiopia's Progress, 1892–1937: the Autobiography of Emperor Haile Selassie I.* Translated and annotated by Edward Ullendorff. London: Oxford University Press, 1976.

———. *Selected Speeches of His Imperial Majesty Haile Selassie I: 1918–1967.* Addis Abeba: Ethiopian Ministry of Information, 1967.

Spencer, John H. *Ethiopia at Bay: A Personal Account of the Haile Selassie Years.* Algonac, MI: Reference Publications, 1984.

Ullendorf, Edward. *The Ethiopians.* London: Oxford University Press, 1965.

Waugh, Evelyn. *Remote People: A Report from Ethiopia and British Africa, 1930–31.* New York: Viking, 1985.

Chronology

July 23, 1892	Born Tafari Makonnen in Ejarsa Goro, Harer province, Ethiopia
1895	Italy invades Ethiopia
1896	Menelik II defeats the Italian army at Adowa
1899	Menelik II conquers the Ogaden region
Nov. 1, 1905	Tafari Makonnen given the title dejazmatch by his father, Ras Makonnen
March 21, 1906	Ras Makonnen dies
March 3, 1910	Tafari appointed governor of Harer province
Dec. 12, 1913	Menelik II dies
Sept. 1916	Empress Zauditu takes power following a coup; Tafari Makonnen named a ras and regent
1923	Ras Tafari successfully petitions for Ethiopia's acceptance into the League of Nations
1928	Tafari forces Zauditu to name him negus
Nov. 2, 1930	Following the death of Zauditu, Ras Tafari Makonnen is crowned emperor of Ethiopia; takes the throne-name Haile Selassie
1931	Ethiopia's first constitution promulgated
1935	Mussolini invades Ethiopia
1936	Haile Selassie flees Ethiopia; addresses the League of Nations; settles into exile in Bath, England
Jan. 1941	British invasion army defeats Italian forces; Haile Selassie returns to Ethiopia
1944	British government restores Haile Selassie as emperor
1952	Eritrea federated with Ethiopia following UN adoption of a U.S.-initiated plan
1955	Revised constitution promulgated
1960	Mengistu Neway, commander of the Imperial Guard, and his brother, Germame mount an unsuccessful coup
1962	Haile Selassie successfully abolishes the federation of Eritrea and Ethiopia
1963	The Organization of African Unity (OAU) is established at a meeting in Addis Abeba
1973	Famine strikes in the northern provinces of Welo and Tigre; Ethiopian government attempts to cover up the famine; high inflation resulting from a sudden rise in oil prices causes major demonstrations by an already frustrated urban population
1974	Haile Selassie overthrown in a popular uprising later coopted by the military
Sept. 12, 1974	Haile Selassie seen in public for the last time
Aug. 28, 1975	Ethiopian radio announces the death of Haile Selassie I

Index

Askale Negash was born and raised in Haile Selassie's Ethiopia. She is currently doing graduate work in history and political science in New York City.

Arthur M. Schlesinger, jr., taught history at Harvard for many years and is currently Albert Schweitzer Professor of the Humanities at City University of New York. He is the author of numerous highly praised works in American history and has twice been awarded the Pulitzer Prize. He served in the White House as special assistant to Presidents Kennedy and Johnson.